COACHING
BEYOND

COACHING BEYOND

MY DAYS *with the* INDIAN CRICKET TEAM

R. SRIDHAR
with R. KAUSHIK

RUPA

First published by
Rupa Publications India Pvt. Ltd 2023
7/16, Ansari Road, Daryaganj
New Delhi 110002

Sales Centres:

Prayagraj Bengaluru Chennai
Hyderabad Jaipur Kathmandu
Kolkata Mumbai

P-ISBN: 978-93-5520-884-2
E-ISBN: 978-93-5520-886-6

Third impression 2023

10 9 8 7 6 5 4 3

The moral right of the author has been asserted.

Printed in India

To my family—especially my wife—and my closest friends, thank you for always believing in me. And to my mentors, colleagues and editors who contributed their time and effort for this project.
Thank you for being a part of this.

CONTENTS

FOREWORD

From the time I can remember, R. Sridhar has been a part of my cricketing life. My first interaction with him dates back more than 35 years, when I was an Under-13 cricketer and he was in a higher age group. Our state camps, under Edulji Bujorji 'Eddie' Aibara sir, used to be held at the Gymkhana Grounds in Secunderabad. One of the first seniors to come over voluntarily and devote his time, attention and energy to us youngsters, was Sridhar.

It was my first introduction to the 'giver' that Sridhar is. Over time, we have got to know each other better and it delights me no end to see the kind of strides he has made as a cricketing and life coach. Sridhar has not allowed the grass to grow under his feet. He has constantly strived to learn and improve and get better each day. To me, it comes as no surprise that he has achieved the successes he has in his avatar as coach for the last two decades.

When I graduated out of the Under-13 ranks and gradually progressed towards the state side, Sridhar was a constant presence, thanks to the fact that both of us trained at St John's Cricket Academy in Secunderabad. We would also play against each other when I represented Andhra Bank and he turned out for State Bank of Hyderabad, or when my Ensconse Cricket Club team took on his Hyderabad Blues side in the Hyderabad Cricket Association leagues.

I have vivid memories of the first time I broke into the

Hyderabad Ranji Trophy team. In February 1993, we travelled to Baroda to take on the home side in the pre-quarterfinal when I was just 18. Even though I didn't play that game, I was delighted to be a part of the team that won by 51 runs. Sridhar's left-arm spin accounted for the final wicket of the game when he trapped Rashid Patel in front. For some reason, that picture stands out clearly in my mind.

Sridhar had to perforce operate in the shadows of the excellent Venkatapathi Raju and therefore perhaps didn't play as much for Hyderabad as he would have liked to. But that didn't mean he moped or complained or moaned. He always had time for us juniors in the squad, and after a strenuous training session, we would often go over to his home, which wasn't far from the Gymkhana and where his mother served us hot breakfast with a constant big smile.

Having toiled away for 11 seasons, even though he only played 35 games for the state, Sridhar, as a 30-year-old, decided that it was time for him to pull the plug on his playing career and focus on a future in coaching. I remember being a part of conversations involving us and A. Nandakishore, where Sridhar spoke passionately about coaching, about helping shape young careers.

He didn't just take to coaching; he did so with total and complete commitment. His early coaching skills were honed by Bobji sir (M.V. Narasimha Rao, the Ranji Trophy-winning Hyderabad captain) and John Manoj at St John's Academy. Sridhar juggled the multiple tasks of playing for his employer, of going to the bank to earn his livelihood and of pursuing his love for coaching with such aplomb that you had to admire him for his determination and time-management skills.

To me, the turning point in his coaching career was the move to the National Cricket Academy (NCA) in 2008. Sridhar had already made a name for himself within the Hyderabad cricket circles, but the NCA gave him a more rounded, national profile. His desire to get better at his job and to make a difference to his wards' lives drove him to keep in touch with the rapid developments in cricket coaching. By now, he had become a certified coach-educator too, and every time I went to the NCA with the Indian team for a camp, I'd come away even more impressed with how much Sridhar had added to his repertoire.

He and Bharat Arun forged a strong coaching relationship at the NCA, and when I spent a lot of time at the academy during 2011, rehabbing from my back injury, I saw how much they fed off each other. It came as no surprise that they were at the coaching forefront of India's Under-19 World Cup win in Australia in 2012, and I felt at that point that it was a matter of when rather than whether they both would graduate to being with the senior side.

By 2014, I had a vision of starting my own cricket academy to help young kids realize their dreams. The idea was for it to be pan-Indian and to offer its services to anyone interested in the sport. I could think of no one better than Sridhar to take over as director of operations. I was looking for someone with integrity, knowledge, ability, compassion and empathy, and Sridhar ticked every box. Unfortunately for me, the move didn't happen, but that same year, Sridhar and Arun joined the Indian team as fielding and bowling coaches, respectively. The rest, as they say, is history.

To see Sridhar continue his progression and become one of the top coaches in the world makes me so proud. I know his designation within the Indian set-up was fielding coach, but he is a lot more than that, as everyone who has interacted with him will testify. As he read up more, spoke to people and invested himself entirely in his passion, you could see his confidence rise visibly and that manifested itself in the results he was able to entice from the players.

I consider Sridhar a role model for any aspiring coach. Back in 2008, he had the safety net of a steady income from his bank job. But he had the conviction to quit his job, move to Bangalore and immerse himself in the pursuit of something that he felt was his calling. I wouldn't call it a gamble, but he was moving into uncharted territory and needed to have great courage to take this gutsy step. I am sure he must be thankful to his family that they allowed him to make this significant decision of relocating and throwing their life as they knew it out of kilter. Where he is today owes itself entirely to that call he took all those years back, and is a timely reminder to all of us that if we do things for the right reasons, the results will more often than not take care of themselves.

Through this book, Sridhar has reflected on his seven-year stint with the Indian team. Like he himself says, this is not a technique-heavy book but a dive into the minds of the top players and what has made them and the Indian team tick. I am sure it will make for a fascinating read.

I congratulate Sridhar on his stirring cricketing journey to date and wish him the very best in his future endeavours.

V.V.S. Laxman
Former Indian Test Cricketer
September 2022

PREFACE

Coaching. This eight-letter word has massive connotations in the world of sport. It's a simple yet paradoxically complicated term that is impossible to define. Like everything else in life, it's an evolutionary process. From personal experience, I can assert that its paradigms change depending on which stage of your coaching career you are in and which group of players you are involved with. Over time, you graduate from an instructor to a facilitator to an empowerer in a journey that can at once be fulfilling and frustrating, exasperating and exhilarating.

I wasn't so much a reluctant as an accidental coach. Having made my first-class debut as a 19-year-old left-arm spinner for Hyderabad, I fought hard to nail a permanent place in a spin-heavy team that included stalwarts such as Arshad Ayub, Venkatapathi Raju and Kanwaljit Singh. By the 2000–01 season, I had played just 35 games, and I knew my cricketing career was at a crossroads. I did have a secure livelihood with State Bank of Hyderabad to fall back on.

As sometimes happens in such cases, when one door appeared shut, another opened without warning. V. Manohar, one of the head coaches at St John's Cricket Academy coaching camp, was emigrating to New Zealand and John Manoj, the other head coach, was looking for someone to work with the Under-19 and Under-22 boys, many of whom had represented Hyderabad teams at the age-group level. When John sir approached me, I wasn't sure what to expect, but I wasn't going to die wondering.

I must confess, the first year and a half or so wasn't the most enjoyable. I pretty much ran the nets, that's all, to be honest. I was an instructor, allocating time for batters and the number of deliveries for bowlers—elements that didn't necessarily appeal to me. Each morning, I would wake up secretly hoping for a spell of rain and, therefore, the cancellation of practice sessions. I could have walked away any time, of course, but that wasn't how I was wired.

Without intending to sound dramatic, the turning point arrived when M.V. Narasimha Rao (Bobji sir) came down from Ireland for a short visit. The former India leg-spinner had led the state to its second—and to date last—Ranji Trophy title in 1986–87 but moved to Ireland post retirement. He flew down to Hyderabad every summer, and during his stay, he'd be involved with coaching the younger lot at St John's Camp.

John sir asked me to work with his fellow co-founder of St John's Cricket Academy, M.V. Narasimha Rao, on the 11- and 12-year-old trainees, and that proved to be the game-changer. Bobji sir was an England and Wales Cricket Board level-three certified coach, and interning under him for a month and a half was a great learning experience. During that period, I soaked in as much as I could by watching how he interacted with the wards, how he treated them and the kind of things he told them. From dreading the drudgery of heading to the camp, I was now excited at the thought of waking up and making the short trip from home to catch up with Bobji sir and the kids.

Once Bobji sir returned to Ireland, John sir asked me to continue training with the younger guys, with whom I had by now struck a good rapport. Gradually, their parents started to talk to me more regularly, and I could see just how much trust they had in the coach in me, in this instance. The kids hung on to every word I said. I was overwhelmed by a sense of responsibility and accountability. If I wished to continue in this role, I couldn't afford to give anything but a 100 per cent. Now it was no longer about me.

Having found my calling, in a manner of speaking, I plunged myself completely into the process. I read up as much as I could on all aspects of coaching because I was still a novice myself. I was a huge fan of Bob Woolmer, the South Africa and later Pakistan coach, and I devoured his books. I watched the other coaches closely, and I was fortunate that in 2004, I was among the five people nominated by the Hyderabad Cricket Association to do my Board of Control for Cricket in India (BCCI) level-one coaching course in Chennai.

I was handed charge of the Hyderabad Under-19 team and we won the South Zone title, though I can hardly claim any credit because the quality in the side was immense. By 2007, not only had I completed my level-three course and topped all comers but had also been coaching the state Under-19 side for three years (2004–07). I was confident my coaching career would follow an organic upward path.

To my great shock, I was replaced as the Under-19 coach. With coaching positions in the state senior side too occupied, suddenly I was out in the cold. The euphoria at topping the level-three course was tempered by the harsh reality of finding myself on the outer, though I still had a very comfortable bank job to fall back on.

In despair, I called up Bharat Arun, who was at the National Cricket Academy (NCA), to discuss my predicament. Arun, a former India paceman, would go on to become a major influence in my coaching career. Arun, who spots a silver lining when others see a cloud, told me it was the best thing that could have happened to me. *Really?* I wondered.

A few months later, in January 2008, I received a call from Dav Whatmore, who was the director at the NCA in Bangalore (now

Bengaluru). He checked my availability as a faculty member for the first-ever all-women level-one course conducted by the NCA. I checked my calendar—just kidding!—and told him of course I was available. The head of the course was Dr Kinjal Suratwala, while the batting aspect was handled by Dinesh Nanavati. It was during that camp that I was first assigned the role of teaching fielding. You know the cliché…

It was a wonderful experience, working with a very enthusiastic group. I was now a specialist, so I had to educate myself on my core competencies. It helped that I had been a fairly decent fielder myself, but doing something and helping others do it are completely different things, as I quickly found out.

When you start playing the game, at any age, you are aspirational. As a young kid, you have dreams of playing for the country. I had no aspirations when I first walked into St John's Camp as a 'coach'. But as I moved up the ranks, so to say, my aspirations grew. When I first worked with the young kids at St John's, I developed a passion for coaching. And when I went to the NCA for the first time, it occurred to me that coaching could be a career option.

I returned to the NCA in the summer of 2008 to work with the India 'A' side that was to tour England. At the academy, I worked with sparkling talent—Shikhar Dhawan, Abhishek Nayar, Subramaniam Badrinath and Ravindra Jadeja—and rediscovered the high that playing had given me. A few months down the line, I did the first-ever Under-19 camp, which featured the likes of Manish Pandey, Yuzvendra Chahal, Varun Aaron, K.L. Rahul and Saurabh Tiwary, among others.

I took unpaid leave of absence from my employers during my NCA stints, and when I was absorbed by the academy, I was nudged towards opting for the voluntary retirement scheme by Arun. It was a significant decision because I was shedding the safety net and plunging into the sometimes uncertain world of professional coaching. I am glad things worked out the way they did; my job allowed me to pursue my passion. I felt blessed that I was among those for whom a job wasn't just that.

During my six years at the NCA between 2008 and 2014, I also got intricately involved in teaching. Apart from being the Under-19 fielding coach for four years, I was part of the faculty for more than a hundred coach education courses for the BCCI, teaching mostly fielding and a little bit of bowling. The more I taught the basics to coaches around the country, the more it got ingrained in me and made coaching a lot easier. It taught me the importance of keeping things simple even if one is coaching at the highest level.

For some reason, a refresher course for players-turned-coaches at the NCA in 2011 has stayed freshest in my mind. Several stalwarts from Karnataka were in attendance, while Rahul Dravid was fine-tuning his skills at nets ahead of the tour of England. We requested Rahul to come and talk to the coaches, and one of the first things he said was, 'As a player, you climb up the rungs steadily. You play age-group cricket, club cricket, state juniors, India Under-19, first-class cricket for the state, then the zone, then perhaps India "A" and finally for India. It's a steady, gradual process. I believe the same should apply to coaches as well. You have to start from scratch. Just because one has played 100 first-class games or 50 Tests doesn't necessarily mean you are equipped to straightaway start coaching at the first-class level. The experience gained from making the step-by-step climb is invaluable, I believe.'

Rahul's words struck a chord with me and with each passing day, I recognized the value of his sentiments. With each passing day, my philosophy towards coaching changed. Early on, I believed the success of a coach lay in the results his wards produced on the field of play. Now, past my fiftieth year and after seven uninterrupted years with the Indian national team, my thinking has been rewired. Nothing pleases me more than seeing young men I have worked with turn out to be fine human beings. If they do well on the ground, I consider that an added bonus.

This is a book that's been on my mind for a while. The aim is to share my journey and throw light on certain experiences that I have been privileged to live out. It's not a technical treatise on coaching, or how to coach, but rather a sincere effort at addressing issues that can influence the effectiveness of the men labelled 'coaches'. Beyond a point, coaching is almost entirely about man-management. Or is it?

1

NO MYSTERY TO MASTERY

'Trouble the comfort, comfort the trouble.'

'**M**astery' is a word used very loosely in every sphere of life. Let's face it, no matter how extraordinary one might be, you can never really master a discipline because that would mean you have learnt everything there is to learn. That's not quite possible, is it? Every day, life presents new learnings, new lessons. That being the case, how can individual components not do so?

That being said, there are individuals who stand out for their command over their craft. They might not have mastered their craft for the reasons mentioned above, but there is no denying the fact that they truly are masters. They don't attain that status because they have been blessed or because a miracle has been bestowed upon them. The 10,000-hour theory which holds that the key to achieving true expertise in any skill is simply a matter of practising, admittedly in the correct way, for at least 10,000 hours is common knowledge. It is in putting this knowledge to practise that the trick lies.

There is no secret to success. It doesn't germinate from grand thoughts but through the relentless pursuit of excellence. Through putting in the hard yards away from the probing public eye.

Through marrying aspiration with stubbornness and the burning desire to be the best one can be, not necessarily the best in comparison with the rest. Quite simply, there is no mystery.

To buttress my point, I will fall back on two examples during my association with the Indian cricket team. Coincidentally, both men are from Delhi, though they couldn't be more different than chalk and cheese. I am talking, of course, about Virat Kohli and Rishabh Pant.

Virat: A Man Possessed

Let's discuss Virat first. There isn't much I can add about his ability as a batter that more accomplished wordsmiths haven't presented. What I can say is that I was privy to the effort that went into making Virat the modern master he has become, particularly after the career-defining Test series in England in 2014. I wasn't in England during the Test series, but watching the action unfold on television, I couldn't help but wonder how such a fabulous batter was repeatedly being sucked into playing deliveries outside off stump, especially by James Anderson, the master of swing who was getting the ball to go away from Virat very late.

By then, Virat had played international cricket for six years, and Test cricket for three. He was expected to be the bulwark of Indian batting for the foreseeable future and had done justice to expectations with impressive runs, especially in limited-overs cricket, where his pedigree was well established.

England, though, offers challenges unique and myriad. If you go through the manuals pertaining to technique, you will realize that most of them have been formulated keeping English conditions in mind. That's perhaps because a lot of the original literature emanated from England, but especially for batters from the subcontinent, even today, England is the ultimate test of their skills, their character and their resilience.

A five-Test series is a double-edged sword. Depending on which way you look at it, it either gives you the opportunity to bounce back from an iffy start, or it can weigh you down mentally and lure you into the same errors that undermined you at the very beginning. In Virat's case, the 2014 series offered no respite. There was little time to work on his batting because in a five-Test series, the matches come thick and fast. Between travel and team training, it's impossible to find the time and the energy to focus singularly on technical issues. That isn't ideal, but given how tightly packed the international schedule is, it is inevitable. For a proud competitor like Virat, returns of 134 runs from 10 innings must have been particularly galling. It was under these circumstances that I first met Virat in my capacity as the fielding coach of the national team. Zimbabwe's Duncan Fletcher continued to be the coach, but the BCCI brought Ravi Shastri on board as the team director. Ravi handpicked Sanjay Bangar, Bharat Arun and yours truly to help out with the batting, bowling and fielding side of things, respectively, ahead of the limited-overs leg on that tour. The four of us landed in London the morning after the Test series ended, joined up with the squad at the team hotel and, after breakfast, we all took the bus to Bristol, where the one-day series was scheduled to kick off.

Hardly had I settled down and started to unpack when the phone in my room rang. Virat was at the other end, asking if I could join him for lunch and if I could bring Arun along with me. We already had a good rapport following our trysts at the NCA, and I was eager to catch up with him, lend a shoulder if he so needed and chart the way forward because I knew he wouldn't take this failure lying down.

By the time the three of us—myself, Virat and Arun—left the hotel, all the Indian restaurants in our vicinity had unfortunately closed, so we ended up at a Subway outlet. Soon, as we grabbed our orders and made our way to a table, Virat's sunny disposition disappeared. He was angry with himself, and he was keen to vent to men he trusted. He just wanted to get things off his chest, and Arun and I listened to him patiently and sympathetically when he talked about administrative, off-field niggles that had irked him during the tour.

Once Virat spewed everything out, he calmed down visibly. You could see the steely resolve in his eyes. You didn't actually need him to tell you, 'Never again will this happen to me, I will make sure of that.'

■

I'd like to believe the seeds of Virat's metamorphosis as a batter were sowed during that impromptu luncheon. I had been a big admirer of his character and personality even at that stage, and I remember telling him, 'Whatever else you do, just be yourself. Don't try to change anything about you.' I think that struck a chord with him. He wanted to improve, he wanted to get better exponentially and he did everything he could in that pursuit, but he has remained true to his core self, which in itself is unbelievable.

Virat was always driven, but after that Test series, he became bullheaded. Like an Olympic athlete, he targeted the next four years. You didn't have to be a rocket scientist to figure out what lay in store four years on—another Test tour of England, where he would end up making close to 600 runs.

I was privileged to be witness to that exhilarating journey. I was able to see how hard he worked on his fitness and on his game plan, how he made no compromises when it came to work ethic and how he turned himself into a run-machine. In my opinion, it's a template for every cricketer to pursue excellence, to become a master. However, the most important thing was, he never moved away from being himself. He did the very best he could, in everything he could, every day. Improvement came to him steadily but naturally. He did everything that would make him better.

Naturally enough, he couldn't have done it all on his own. That's where the coaching staff came in; Ravi and Sanjay primarily, and sometimes me as well. Ravi was the one who suggested that Virat stand a little out of his crease and take an off stump guard so that he doesn't go feeling for balls in the fourth- to sixth-stump corridor, apart from opening up the on-side as a fertile scoring option. When you stand on the off stump, you know how wide a ball is and whether it requires you to offer a stroke to it. After all, in Test cricket, the bowlers try to feast on the so-called 'corridor of uncertainty', which the channel outside off is referred to as. It's a game of cat and mouse, with the bowler trying to suck the batter into playing the widish lines and the batter bringing his wisdom and common sense into play to ensure he only plays at those deliveries that he is supremely confident will not lure him to his downfall.

The one thing about Virat is that he is unafraid to experiment in his quest for improvement. He took advice on board and adopted the best practices that suited him. I remember a lot of his conversations with Ravi and Sanjay about where to stand and how to use the crease well because the crease belongs to the batter. He worked specifically on angles and how to counter different angles from which the ball was coming. He ensured his feet were in the right place.

He wanted to be peppered by real short bowling from a short distance to improve his reaction time. His main aim was to move his feet as much as he could, even if the ball came at him at 150 kmph. He wanted to be right there, so that he could go for the ball.

D. Raghavendra (Raghu), one of our throw-down specialists, was thrust with the responsibility of aiding Virat's battle-readiness as we eyed our next overseas tour, towards the end of 2014 in Australia for four Test matches. Now, I am convinced Raghu loves hitting batters. I can see a wicked gleam in his eyes when he does so, though outwardly, he is very contrite and apologetic! Given the licence by Virat himself to go all out, Raghu put him through the wringer, hurling the ball at great pace and offering angles and awkward bounce of the sort Virat could expect to face in the matches ahead. Virat loved the routines. He enjoyed the ball homing in on his helmet at great pace. He didn't mind looking ugly in the nets if that was what it took to stamp his authority in a match-situation.

Virat is as much a creature of habit as anyone else. Especially at the beginning of an away tour, he bats long periods at the nets, in two or three different stints. On average, he plays between 250 and 300 balls a day as he gets used to the pitches, the ball, the atmosphere and the sync between his body and mind. He doesn't fool around at the nets, he hates getting out even in practice. He berates himself at every false shot and is quickly in one of our ears seeking clarification or confirmation on what he did not do right. In that regard, he is a lot like Sachin Tendulkar, though I never had the honour of working with the great man as part of the Indian team. Once the Tests start, however, Virat's time in the nets tapers off. He has short, crisp sessions, where he focusses on specifics and for reassurance that the ball is leaving his bat nicely. He does have an issue with getting himself up for warm-up games, which is understandable because the stakes aren't high and Virat is the kind of guy who is always at his intense best, no matter what match he is playing. From a coaching staff point of view, we'd rather he reserve his energies for international matches than practice ties.

By the time we went to Australia that winter of 2014, Virat was ready. He had warmed up nicely with a few good outings against West Indies at home, though the tour was called off midway through following a pay dispute between the players and the West Indies board. While he would have loved the opportunity to play matches, Virat didn't miss any chance to put in the hard yards at the nets. That was evident on what would have been our first day of international action with the Indian team in Bristol. The game was washed out, but we immediately hit the nets. While Duncan's wisdom was most welcome, Virat enjoyed Ravi's presence too, because the two of them share a similar competitive, never-take-a-backward-step streak.

One of the great coaching lines I love is: 'Trouble the comfort, comfort the trouble.' As self-explanatory as that might seem, let me dwell on it a little. Not all players willingly attempt to get out of their comfort zones. They need to be goaded into putting themselves in situations where they are not comfortable, so that they can maximize their abilities. Likewise, some others find it very difficult to find a certain equilibrium. They might end up putting too much pressure on themselves and beating themselves up over little things. In those cases, it becomes our responsibility to alleviate their troubles and get them to a certain level of comfort, from where they can build their confidence back and get into more challenging scenarios. With Virat, that has never been an issue. Nothing gets his juices flowing more than being asked the toughest questions and being put in the most demanding situations. If they didn't happen organically, then he demanded those arduous tasks because he didn't want to leave anything to chance. One of the main reasons for his overwhelming success post 2014 is his attention to minute detail and exemplary preparedness that ensures he remains unfazed, no matter what.

In theory, it is reasonably easy to want to bat out of your crease, but imagine doing so on the quicker, bouncier tracks in Australia against an express paceman, which Mitchell Johnson was in 2014–15. The first ball Virat received in that series was a bouncer from Johnson, which clattered into his helmet. It was the moment of truth, the moment of reckoning. Virat responded like only he can, not just during that innings or that Test but throughout the series, which he finished with four centuries. He stunned Australia with his audacity and his range of strokes. As we know, it was not as if suddenly, he flipped a switch on and everything fell into place. All his hard work of the preceding few months had finally paid off. That reaffirmed his commitment to the power of preparation, to the relentless work culture that was soon to rub off on the rest of his mates.

Those four years (2014–18) between the two tours of England saw Virat bat like a man possessed. He kept raising the bar, putting the past behind him. Never mind if he had made 10 or 200 in the previous innings, he remained hungry and greedy, which manifested itself in a mountain of mellifluous runs he made.

Before that England series, we were in South Africa in January 2018 preparing for a Test series. They had given us a county ground for practice. The pitches were horrible. There was one centre wicket on which we were practising, but the side wickets at Western Province in Cape Town were far from ideal. Virat saw that nobody was batting on the wicket because it could be a bit dangerous. He quickly padded up, called Sanjay, Raghu and myself and said he wanted to bat. We tried to dissuade him, but he was adamant he wanted to bat on that surface. 'I want it to be dangerous, I want to bat on this dangerous wicket and I want Raghu to bowl at his fastest.' That is what he did. He did that every time. He put himself under severe distress in difficult conditions and ensured he overcame it. So, as he was honing his skill, he was also sharpening himself mentally.

Let me talk about another instance to reiterate his passion and total dedication to the sport. In March 2021, we were in Ahmedabad for the third of four Tests against England. It was our first sighting of the Narendra Modi Stadium, which would be hosting only the second day–night Test in India. We were not guaranteed a place in the final of the World Test Championship (WTC), so there was a lot riding on this match. Much debate had been generated by how the colour of the seats, many of which would be unoccupied due to the restrictions necessitated by the pandemic, could offer a difficult backdrop against which to sight the pink ball.

Virat knew he could not control anything else beyond being ready for the unexpected. So, he tugged me aside for a fielding session in twilight under a not-so-ideal backdrop of orange chairs that dotted the stands, taking close to an unbelievable 200 catches. And that too, the night before a Test match! Shubman Gill, who was looking on from a distance, eventually got so tired of watching that he too decided to join in the fun. Virat smiled at him cheekily and said, 'I am giving you 10 years in age, young man. The least you can do is take a few catches yourself.' The session only ended when, in exasperation, the manager came out to inform him that the rest of the squad was ready and good to go and that the team bus was leaving for the hotel in 10 minutes.

So, there you have it, the mystery to Virat's mastery. It's a blueprint every aspiring youngster would do well to commit to memory and try to emulate.

Rishabh: A Promising Genius

Rishabh Pant has taken a while finding his feet in international cricket, but before we are too harsh on him, it is worth remembering that he is a very young man whose precocious talent thrust him into the public glare when he was only a teenager. I have been witness to his journey at the highest level from day one, and it warms my heart to see the giant strides he has taken and the stature he has attained, especially since the start of 2021.

Such was the promise he showed, particularly with the bat, that he was inducted into the Indian T20 XI as far back as February 2017 as a specialist batter, when M.S. Dhoni was still going strong. I distinctly remember Rishabh's debut in Bengaluru against England, where at No. 6, he only got to play three deliveries. I also recall the excellent catch he held in the deep to get rid of Eoin Morgan, the England captain. He covered good ground to his right from deep mid-wicket and slid on his knees to gobble up the offering—the first indication that he wasn't out of his depth in or overawed by the international stage.

While much of the talk outside centred round his electric batting, we were convinced he was the long-term successor to MS in all formats as wicketkeeper-batter. His keeping was fairly basic at the time, if I may say so. That is not an indictment of the coaching he had received, or his own abilities, because the bowlers he had kept to till that point weren't all world class and he did what was required of him at the time.

From the way he moved and threw himself around, it was obvious that he was very explosive as a keeper too, but he was also unorthodox in the sense that he didn't follow the basics to a T. The insistence on basics is to get an impeccable skeletal structure in place, on which one can improvise. With Rishabh, because he was a unique version, it took a lot of work and plenty of adjustments before he could evolve into the excellent gloveman he is today.

Till such time that MS was around, Rishabh had to bide his time in white-ball cricket, and we felt he wasn't yet ready for Test cricket, not until the tour of England in 2018. The India 'A' team was touring England at the same time and midway through the series, Rishabh was called up to the Test squad on the back of impressive runs for India 'A'. He made an excellent debut in the third Test in Nottingham with five catches in his first innings behind the stumps—a lot of credit to the bowlers for finding the edges—and rounded off the tour with a memorable maiden 100 in the final game at The Oval. When we got back home, he made runs against West Indies, but clearly, he found it difficult to keep to the exceptional spin duo of Ravichandran Ashwin and Ravindra Jadeja. Again, that was no reflection on his skill. The promise was immense, but he had had very little experience of keeping to such high-quality spinners on Indian pitches that assisted them a bit, and where the bounce was a little low. However, another sign that he had the wisdom to delink his two primary disciplines came when he made 90s in both Tests.

Largely because of his electric batting and because the tracks in Australia wouldn't test his keeping too much, Rishabh started the historic four-Test series in 2018–19 and proved his worth with the bat in spectacular fashion. He rounded off a consistent tour with a brilliant unbeaten 159 in the drawn final Test in Sydney— a result that formalized our first series triumph Down Under.

Despite all this, we weren't unaware that Rishabh was still a work-in-progress. There was so much to be done if he was to become a top-notch wicketkeeper in India. The tour of the Caribbean in 2019, not long after the World Cup, was where the wheels were seriously set in motion.

After the tour of the West Indies, we were scheduled to play home series against South Africa and Bangladesh, and we had pretty much decided that Wriddhiman Saha, man-for-man the best wicketkeeper in the world at the time, would slot in for those five Tests. The idea was to allow Rishabh to grow and evolve as a keeper without having the weight of the world on his shoulders, which would have been the case had he kept in the home Tests and made mistakes any keeper might have.

Rishabh worked really hard for the next seven or so months, and you could see that he was a better, more confident mover. However, there were still inputs he was a little reluctant to take on board, because he trusted the game that had brought him to this level. Sometimes, I must confess, it drove me nuts, his stubbornness. But getting angry or frustrated wasn't going to help anyone. I had to find a way to get Rishabh to try to do different things, if only for him to figure out if those changes might actually be beneficial to his keeping.

I fell back on another of my favourite coaching maxims: 'If they don't like what you coach, coach them what they like.' Actually, that's not exactly what I did, I modified it a little.

We were in New Zealand in January 2020 for a full tour, and Rishabh was to return to the Test XI after missing the home games. We spent a lot of time together at practice, often just him and me, and I decided it was time for a little tough love. I stopped giving suggestions and inputs, and would ignore his quizzical looks when the ball burst through his hands or he fumbled with his collections. Rishabh has the smarts, so it didn't take him long to work out that something wasn't quite right. I suspect he thought I was angry with him, which I probably was in an oblique way, but more than that, I wanted him to come up with questions rather than keep plying him with advice that, in any case, was sailing over his head.

We were working on a specific drill, full balls pitched outside the leg stump. Rishabh would stop or parry all of them, but only a small percentage would actually nestle in his gloves. More than once, I was tempted to tell him something, but I remembered what I had set out to do. After a while, he walked up to me and said, '*Kya, Sir, aap kuch bhi nahi bol rahen hain. Batayiye na, mein kya karoon* (Sir, you aren't saying anything. Please tell me what to do).' Smiling inwardly, I replied in Hindi to the tune of, 'Maybe you should lead with your head rather than with your hands.' Satisfied at having got me to shed my silence, he went back and did precisely that. As the head led the way, so did the body move to his left, and he was more assured in gathering the ball with his hands close to the body. I'd like to believe that was the first turning point in his evolution as a wicketkeeper; he realized that there was another way of doing things that would be to his betterment. Since then, whatever trust deficit there might have been has disappeared, and I am glad I have never had to subject him to the silent treatment again.

Throughout the length of the New Zealand tour, we spent long hours fine-tuning various aspects of his wicketkeeping. Rishabh was now a willing learner, trying out all my suggestions, accepting those that worked for him and leaving some out that he felt didn't really suit his style. That was fine by me because I wanted him to think about what he was doing, not merely continue to rigidly follow the same set routines he was hooked to.

Rishabh had made considerable progress as a gloveman when the pandemic brought cricket to a standstill. We would be constantly in touch—our relationship had attained a new dynamic—but clearly, with the lockdown in place, he had nowhere to practise. Even so, I was a little surprised when I saw him on television at the start of the delayed Indian Premier League (IPL) in the United Arab Emirates (UAE). He looked rusty but more damagingly, physically out of shape. Perhaps subconsciously, he had neglected his body, and consequently had put on a few kilos more than where we wanted him to be.

When I met him in the UAE a month and a half later, ahead of the tour of Australia, I realized that he still had plenty of weight to shed. By now, he had lost his place in the white-ball squad, and that hurt a lot, he admitted to me. I told him simply, 'It's up to you how you want to channelize that hurt. You know that a little hard work goes a long way.'

In so many ways, his omission from white-ball cricket was a blessing in disguise. It gave us time to work almost exclusively on his wicketkeeping. Rishabh was happy to not spend too much time batting in the nets if it meant more attention to his keeping skills. We tried to simulate the conditions we would most likely face in India because we wanted him to be a part of the Test series against England, especially with a place in the final of the WTC at stake.

So, we roughed up the business area of pitches. We would drape a rope across the width of the pitch and target that rope. Once the ball landed on the rope, there was no gainsaying which direction it would deviate in. That tested his reflexes more than his anticipation. We used all kinds of balls—tennis, plastic, dimpled bowling-machine balls, the conventional cricket ball—and changed up lengths. The rough helped generate uneven bounce. Watching Rishabh go at it, I could feel his desperation. Looking at how charged up he was reminded me of Virat in the immediacy of the England tour of 2014.

A couple of days before the first Test in Adelaide, Rishabh asked me if he was slated to play the game. I knew he wasn't, but it wasn't my place to tell him that. Instead, I said, 'I am not 100 per cent sure. Why don't you ask Ravi bhai?' Ravi told him that he wasn't starting the series; already hurting at being left out of the limited-overs set-up, this steeled his resolve further. He worked his backside off, both in the gym and on the park, and came armed with a series of questions.

One of the biggest challenges for Rishabh was to keep his weight on the balls of his feet while getting up to receive the ball. Invariably, he would be balanced on the heels, which reduced his efficacy considerably. I told him to keep his hands a little in front of his body, so that when he got up, the weight would automatically push him forward and he would be on the balls rather than the heels of his feet. It didn't take him long to perfect that technique.

By the second Test in Australia, Rishabh had taken his place behind the sticks, but not for once did I worry if the work we had done with India specifically in mind would affect his keeping in Australia. In my opinion, Australia is the easiest place to keep wicket. The bounce is true, there isn't any great lateral movement and the ball definitely doesn't do crazy things after passing the stumps, like in England. Unsurprisingly, Rishabh was tidy and composed behind the stumps. More influentially, he was outstanding in front of it, nearly setting up an extraordinary chase in Sydney in a match we did remarkably well to draw in the end. In further reiteration of his coming of age as a Test cricketer, Rishabh masterminded a record chase in Brisbane to help India pull off a glorious, against-the-odds victory and complete our second series win in a row in Australia. The confidence in his wicketkeeping had rubbed off on his batting. The pain of being benched had been used constructively when the young man could have allowed himself to wallow in self-pity.

By the time we returned to India with the Border–Gavaskar Trophy, and with our heads held high after one of the most sensational coups in Test history, I was sure Rishabh would pass the home test with flying colours. His improvement was neither dramatic nor ephemeral; it had been gradual and exponential. It wasn't a miracle that he was starting to keep well. He had given it his everything day after day, for nearly two months. I knew he was ready for Ashwin and the left-arm spinners, whether the ball turned or bounced or crept along the carpet. Rishabh had bridged the gap between potential and performance through sheer dint of desire. I had seen him put in the hard yards. I was convinced he would reap the rewards very soon.

Rishabh's keeping in the four Tests against England was unbelievable to most, but not for us, who knew what had gone on behind the scenes. He was compact, he moved beautifully, he was swift on his feet, superbly balanced, and his hands never went anywhere without the head and body for company. I allowed myself a quiet smile when heaps of praise were showered on him. Those not privy to the goings-on in practice were both amazed and impressed by Rishabh's sudden improvement, but as we know, there was nothing sudden about it.

In as much as Rishabh was able to separate his batting and his keeping in the infancy of his Test career, he has now found a happy medium where he can feed off success in one discipline to thrive in the other. If further evidence was required of how long he has traversed as the real deal in Test cricket, it came in the final game in Ahmedabad. We were hanging on by the skin of our teeth in a match we could not afford to lose when, in a roaring counterattack with the phlegmatic Washington Sundar (Washi) for company, Rishabh ripped England to shreds. He knew exactly what he was doing. There was no wild slogging, no having a go at every ball. He picked his spots and targeted bowlers astutely. There was as much method to his batting as to his keeping, and there was an inevitability to his first century on home turf. In the space of two months and six Tests, he had played three incredible knocks to haul India to the WTC final. Oh, and amidst all this, his wicketkeeping was of the highest order. The sky truly is the limit for this charismatic, fun-loving bloke whose cheerful exterior effectively masks the resilience and fire that is a must to succeed at the highest level.

2

THAT WINNING CULTURE

'For every gaali they give, we will have to give three gaalis. For every bouncer they bowl, we will have to bowl three bouncers...'

India's entry into the final of the WTC in 2021 was neither a dramatic nor an overnight development. It was the culmination of the work put in over the last six years or so, with the first seeds sowed towards the end of 2014, when Virat was temporarily in charge of the Test team in Adelaide because MS was injured.

By then, it was obvious that Virat would be the natural successor to India's most successful skipper at that moment, though no one was aware that MS would drop the Test retirement bombshell midway through that tour of Australia, in December 2014.

It's no accident that we have finished as the year-end No. 1 Test team for five consecutive years, between 2016 and 2021. They say getting to the top is easier than staying there. It has been a hard grind, both getting to the pinnacle and then continuing to occupy that position—not a mean accomplishment in an era where all three formats compete for eyeballs and participation, and where players' mental and physical reserves are stretched too thin.

The sustained success of the team is testament to the culture of inclusiveness and fearlessness that has been an integral part of our game plan since 2014, which is my reference point because that's when I joined the set-up. It was a culture espoused by the captain and heartily endorsed by the coach, two kindred spirits whose strong bond of mutual respect and admiration was tinged with a steely resolve and a never-back-down mindset.

The 2014–15 tour of Australia was my first full-fledged outing with the Indian team. We were due to fly out from Mumbai a little after the BCCI Awards night, after which we would retire to our rooms, change into our travel gear and head out for the airport. Instinctively, Ravi called for a quick meeting after the function before we dispersed for our rooms.

'Look,' he started, without preamble, 'I have been going to Australia for a long time and I have seen how they play their cricket. If we go there and play cricket the same way as we have been earlier, there is not much we will bring back to India. We are not going to win Jack. For every step they take, we will have to take two steps forward. For every gaali they give, we will have to give three gaalis. For every bouncer they bowl, we will have to bowl three bouncers, not only on the field but even off it. The only way we can beat Australia is with aggression. I don't want no timid guys taking that flight.' The instructions were clear-cut, the message was very clear—we will take the bull by its horns. Whether we win or lose didn't matter, we would not play timid cricket. That suited Virat perfectly, as we were to soon find out.

Adelaide was the precursor to what the cricket world could expect from new India. Australia had built on a useful first-innings lead by pulling away to 290 for five at the end of the fourth day of the first Test, an overall lead of 363. We knew a declaration was imminent, if not overnight then very early on the final morning.

After our warm-downs, we were in the process of packing up when word filtered through that Ravi and Virat wanted to have a quick chat, a quick huddle in the dressing room. Virat was filling the captaincy breach caused by the injury to MS, who was on tour with us and would be available from the second Test. In his first outing as Test captain, Virat was unequivocal in what India's approach would be the next morning. 'No matter what target they set us, we are going to chase it down.' We were already looking at a required rate of four an over in case Australia declared overnight, which they did. But Virat was unshakeable in his belief that there was no question of battening down the hatches and looking for a draw.

Virat later told me that on the bus ride back to the hotel, MS slid into the seat next to him. 'Look, Virat, you can chase down this total, you are that kind of a player and we all know that. But as captain, you will also have to think about what the others are capable of,' MS told him. 'Can they do it? Are the other batters capable of playing that positively and attempting to chase down 360 on the final day of a Test match? While making decisions, you will have to consider the strength of the entire team.'

Virat said he saw some merit in what MS had said, but he was clear in his mind that positivity was the way forward. Virat's reply to MS was pithy, 'Only if we try can we know na? Whether they can do it or not... We have not chased 360 on the last day of a Test match ever before because we haven't yet tried to do that. Let us try and give it a shot. Unless we try, how will we know how good we are?'

As we had anticipated, Australia declared overnight and our target was 364. For large parts of the chase, with Virat and Murali Vijay at the forefront, we were well on course and we could see that Australia were rattled. We had reached 242 for two at one stage, within sight of the finishing tape, when Nathan Lyon got into the act. Despite Virat's second 100 of the Test, we went down by 46 runs, but to me, that match was the beginning of where the Indian Test team is today. That was the moment we knew as a team that this is how we are going to play Test cricket going ahead under the captaincy of Virat Kohli.

As destiny would have it, Virat became captain in his own right for the final Test in Sydney when MS announced his Test retirement after steering the side to a draw in Melbourne. By now, Virat had his concerns over Cheteshwar Pujara's rate of scoring—one of the reasons why Pujara lost his place in the XI for the Sydney Test. Our next series was the tour of Sri Lanka in August that year, and Pujara was dropped for the first two Tests there too. Virat, and all of us, wanted a better strike rate from him because we wanted the game to go forward. We also spoke to Pujara about that, and while I wouldn't say he went from a Rolls-Royce to a Ferrari, there was a marked show of intent when he returned in an unfamiliar role as opener in the series decider at the Sinhalese Sports Club ground in Colombo.

In that period between January and August 2015, Pujara understood what the team needed from him. He understood what he needed to do to secure himself a place, first of all, and what he had to do to align his approach with that of the team's. From there on, Pujara started to play at a slightly better strike rate. He started using his feet better, making technical changes. He has not looked back thereafter and has been an integral part of the team since 2016.

Beyond the obvious, the reason Virat and Ravi wanted Pujara to score faster was because they were sure he had the skill set to do it. It was a question of convincing him that he could do so at the international level. If he needed bollocking occasionally, Ravi was happy to oblige, like in Visakhapatnam in October 2019.

We were looking for quick runs in the second innings, so that we could stick South Africa back in. Rohit Sharma, who had got a 100 in the first innings, was again flowing, but Pujara got stuck. At one stage, he was eight off 61 deliveries when Ravi decided he had seen enough. So, he called one of the sub fielders and instructed him to repeat his message to Pujara verbatim, 'Stop riding a f***ing Luna and get on a Harley-Davidson.' There was a passage of play just after that where Pujara actually outscored Rohit! He had the capability; it was important to ensure his thoughts were always aligned to that of the team and to make him realize that he had the tools to do so.

■

If Adelaide had been the starting point, the big turnaround came in Galle, in the first Test of that Sri Lanka series. Not without reason is it said that the best lessons come from disappointments and adversity.

We played an almost flawless Test for the first two days. We got Sri Lanka out cheaply and amassed a big total on the back of centuries from Shikhar and Virat. With a lead of 192, we were eyeing a handsome victory after reducing Lanka to 92 for five in the second innings, but the game drifted away from us in one session when Dinesh Chandimal went hammer and tongs. We didn't have the best of game plans and Chandimal punished us with a spectacular counterattacking 169. It meant instead of an innings win, we had to chase down 176, which, even on a turner, should have been straightforward for our line-up, and especially with Virat batting like a run-hungry machine.

We ended day three on 23 for the loss of K.L. Rahul's wicket, and I think that evening, we removed our eyes from the process and started thinking about the result. We went back to the hotel and believed that we would get the runs the next day, that we would be 1-0 up sometime before tea. Instead of placing our entire focus on the process of getting the remaining 150-odd runs, on how to play Rangana Herath or how to counter them on a turning Galle surface, what the shot-making options were and where to get the runs, we just took it for granted that we would get home. We were so confident of reaching our target that the required game planning did not happen.

Sure enough, the next morning, Herath brought all his experience and familiarity with the Galle strip into play and spun us out with a seven-for. We were shell-shocked—not sure where the runs would come from, not sure what strokes to pull out. In the end, we were well beaten by 63 runs. It was a heavy defeat, a crushing defeat that hurt—*really* hurt.

For an hour after the final ball was bowled, not a word was uttered in the dressing room. You could have heard a pin drop, so heavy was the air with mourning and disappointment. Then, Ravi roused himself up and thundered, 'All right, guys, we are not leaving this dressing room till we shed our inhibitions. We must clearly define how we want to play Test cricket moving forward. If I have anything to do with it, and I do [he was the team director then, solely in charge with Duncan's term having ended with the World Cup], we are not playing timid Test match cricket like we did in this innings. We need to clearly define how we want to be known as a Test team.'

That opened the floodgates. There was honest soul-searching, everyone spoke their heart out, and talking was mandatory—no one had the option of not speaking. Virat spoke passionately of his vision and what he wanted to do and how he wanted to do that. After a good two hours of brainstorming, we decided two things were non-negotiable so far as the Indian team was concerned. First was to be absolutely fearless. Second was to be brutally honest—to yourself, your teammates and the coaching staff.

We wanted to play a fearless brand of cricket. When you play Test cricket, there will be moments when you will need to be cautious, there will be moments where you may have to be conservative and there will be moments when you will have to be courageous. On most occasions, we agreed, our brand of play should be between caution and courage. We will never ever become conservative. Those were the three Cs we spoke about.

At the bottom of our graph was conservatism, somewhere in the middle was caution and at the peak of the graph was courage. We wanted to be somewhere between caution and courage, depending on the game situation, the conditions and the opposition. In cricket, there will be moments where discretion is the better part of valour. But this is how we wanted to play, be courageous and use caution as Plan B. As much as that, we told ourselves that our focus must be on the process, there should be no compromise on that.

We lost in Galle because we didn't sweep Herath, the orthodox left-arm spinner, nor did we use our feet and step out of the crease to tackle him. And suddenly, we didn't know where to get the runs from. We thought they would come, but how would they unless we had a game plan? Obviously, all cricket teams go through this at some stage or the other, probably that was the brain freeze for our entire squad, including the support staff. That's when we decided: let's do what we can at this time. Winning became our mantra. It was a reaffirmation of how thinking about the process is more important than thinking about the outcome. Galle had laid bare the pitfalls of thinking about the outcome and ignoring the process. After that game, we reversed that, we reversed that very quickly, and that showed the character of the team. Remember, all the established stars now were at least 50 Tests lighter in terms of experience at that stage.

True to our new-found philosophy, we fought back outstandingly from the heartbreak in Galle to complete India's first series win in Sri Lanka since 1993. Ashwin's bowling in that series and the overall batting was brilliant. That 2-1 result was definitely the point when the team culture was defined—that that's how we are going to play going forward. There were no two ways about it, everyone had to buy into it.

Fielding didn't become an option either after that series. We got together and decided fielding wasn't something you practised only if you felt like it. Whether you want to do it or not, it has to be on par with batting and bowling. It can't be that I am not batting, I am not bowling, so I will take a few catches. No, not any more. Everyone had to do their catching drills.

We were training at the Adelaide Oval in January 2016, the day before the start of the three-match Twenty20 International (T20I) series against Australia. I was putting Virat through the grind and, typically, he held nothing back. Yuvraj Singh (Yuvi) walked past me when I had expected him to join in and sat himself down in the dugout, watching us intently. Once Virat had left the field a few minutes later, Yuvi came across for his practice. He told me, 'I couldn't have kept pace with Virat or matched his intensity. I thought it best that I leave you guys to it and once he is finished, I can work on my fielding at my own pace.' I could see where he was coming from. The next day, Yuvi held a blinder at short cover off Hardik Pandya to get rid of Chris Lynn. There is something to say for practising at one's own pace, I guess.

Test cricket is all about catching. No matter how much you practise, you won't be at your best all the time, you will still drop catches. But let us give ourselves the best chance of getting the job done. From then on, it became literally compulsory for each player to get his fielding and catching done with the same intensity as his core discipline.

Another positive and far-reaching fallout was the seismic shift in our thinking with regard to team composition. It was in the despair of Galle that lay the genesis of the five-bowler theory. We realized that if we wanted to win Test matches, it could only happen if we took 20 wickets. So, we moved to the five-bowler theory on most occasions. Yes, we have played four bowlers from time to time, but playing five bowlers had another advantage. It put more emphasis on the top-five batters and made them more accountable. They had to take responsibility and that is what made them better batters. We knew five bowlers provided us with a better option of winning Test matches, both at home and abroad, and while we did occasionally switch back to four bowlers, five specialist bowlers became the norm rather than the exception post that Sri Lanka series.

Hearteningly, from the point of view of us coaches, everyone in the team was on the same page. Everyone wanted to play that brand of cricket. They were looking forward to a different approach to the sport. Since most of them were Virat's contemporaries, they had known for a while that when he took over as captain, this was what was going to happen. Once they bought into it as a group, it was more than half the job done. Virat didn't have to sell it. That afternoon in Galle, this was an agreed decision taken and most of the guys in Southampton for the WTC final were there in Galle that day. That was probably a decision everyone wanted. Gradually, word started spreading within Indian cricketing circles, and those aspiring to play for the country knew this is how we were going to approach matches. That we were going to score at a certain rate, we were going to be fearless. That we were going to be honest in assessing our game and what our thinking would be while deciding a playing XI.

What that meant was that when new guys came in, they already knew what they had to do. They didn't have to be hand-held and sat down and told exactly what the culture of the team was. In any case, MS had already established a tradition of making the newest member feel both important and welcome. Whenever we won a trophy, he would immediately give it to the newest addition, as most of you would have seen on television or in group pictures.

While they were aware of the culture, when they came in, their roles were clearly defined in terms of what we expected from them. I'd like to go back to England in 2018 to offer an example of the culture of inclusivity I have spoken of.

After the third Test of the series, Prithvi Shaw and Hanuma Vihari came into the squad for the first time on the back of phenomenal performances for India 'A'. They joined the team in Southampton, and almost immediately after they checked in, we all went out for lunch—the two new boys, Ravi, Virat, Arun and me.

At lunch, Virat did most of the talking. Ravi chimed in from time to time and I could visibly see the nerves and tension disappear from Prithvi and Vihari. As is understandable, they must have come with their fair share of apprehensions. They were feeling the waters for the first time, trying to get a sense of the temperature of the Indian team. To be sought out by their captain on the first day and being asked out to lunch instantly freed up their minds.

One of the first lessons they received was to take practice as seriously as if it were a match. Virat spoke to them about how to prepare for practice. As a batter, when you wake up in the morning, you should think of the bowlers you will face at nets that day and devise a game plan to tackle them.

Something he said stands out very clearly in my head: 'Hard work doesn't know who is working hard.' What he meant was that if you work hard, if you have prepared well, there is no way you are not going to achieve success. He also spoke about imbibing the 'I will do it when the best can't do it' attitude—that if Virat, Cheteshwar and Ajinkya Rahane are not able to fetch runs, then I will get them.

That is the attitude we wanted in the youngsters coming in, that is how we broke them in. Virat stressed to the two young lads the importance of searching for an opportunity in every ball at the crease—that is how the game moves forward. You've got to move the game forward every ball, whether you are batting or fielding, at every opportunity. Your demands depend on your mindset. What you want from yourself, what you want from the game, depends on your mindset. Then he spoke to them about how to balance the mind and the emotions and what happens when the mind gets ahead of the game. He cited his own example of 2014 and 2018, when he was in the middle of a purple patch. He said Test cricket was all about that clarity.

'In 2014, I didn't have that clarity—where my runs would come from, what my game plan was, but in this series, I have clarity,' he told the two wide-eyed young men. 'I know where to stand to [James] Anderson, where he would bowl to me, what kind of shots I could play. Not just batting, Test cricket needs to be filled with clarity, which comes from being in the present and focussing on the things you do.' That is how youngsters were introduced to the team. And they knew straightaway that since it was coming from the leader himself, this was precisely what the team wanted of them too. It's the same with the young bowlers coming in. Every youngster breaking through was given an induction, on most occasions by the captain or the head coach. Sometimes, one of the other coaches took over.

Not long back, Suryakumar Yadav broke into the Indian team on the strength of his domestic performances for Mumbai and for his franchises in the IPL. We were in the middle of a fielding drill when he suddenly asked me, 'Sir, how am I doing? How is my fielding?' I looked him in the eye and replied, 'Look, Surya, I am not going to teach you how to field. You are already a top fielder and we both know it. My job here is to align you and your skills with the requirements of the team. This is the team culture...this is how we are going to approach fielding in T20 cricket, one-day cricket or Test cricket. This is what we are doing. These are your skills. You have to align them in a manner that is in the best interest of the team. If your intent and thought process is not in tune with what the team wants, I will tell you that this attitude is not acceptable. In this team, that won't work. If you bring the right attitude and work ethic into the environment, then my job becomes very easy.' Most of the times, when youngsters came in—and Indian youngsters being Indian youngsters, they came in with a lot of skill sets—they had the potential. As a coach, my task was to ensure those skill sets were precisely what the team required of them.

It's easy to say this is our team culture and we will stick to it, but it's equally important for the newcomers to realize that there is a reason for this culture, there is a reason why we required them to embrace it. That's why we encouraged them to give their inputs, to speak their mind, because it was a very inclusive environment. We loved young bowlers walking up and talking to those who had been around for six or seven years because we believed in reverse learning. It is inevitable that senior cricketers have baggage; a youngster comes in without baggage. He brings a certain kind of freshness because he doesn't have baggage from a previous encounter with the same bowler or batter. He doesn't have baggage of a previous encounter at the same venue. Sometimes, listening to them brings a different and much fresher perspective. Much of our coaching style revolves around asking questions. What do you think? What are you going to do in this situation? How do you see this situation? They are allowed to give their perspective because it is laced with a certain amount of innocence. And that perspective might actually be the one that makes the most sense.

That doesn't mean it is hunky-dory all the time. Like in any family, there will be differences of opinion. I personally feel it is good to have different voices and different views, but the trick is to ensure these differences don't snowball into unpleasantness. After the 2019 World Cup, for instance, there was a lot of bad press about what allegedly happened in the dressing room during our campaign and following our loss to New Zealand in the semifinal. We were informed that there was a Rohit camp and a Virat camp, that someone had unfollowed another on social media—stuff that could be unsettling if you allowed it to fester.

We landed in the United States (US) some 10 days after the World Cup for a T20 series against West Indies in Lauderhill. One of the first things Ravi did on arrival was to call Virat and Rohit to his room and impress upon them that for Indian cricket to be healthy, they had to be on the same page. 'Whatever happened on social media, that's all fine, but you two are the most senior cricketers, so this must stop,' Ravi said in his typical, no-nonsense manner. 'I want you to put all this behind and get together for us to move forward.'

You could see that things started to get better after that. Ravi's action was swift, simple and decisive. It was just getting both the guys together, sitting them down and making them talk. Ravi didn't waste any time in doing so. That he felt encouraged to call the white-ball captain and his deputy to clearly state his mind is indicative of the kind of atmosphere we had facilitated. That Virat and Rohit saw reason in Ravi's stance and immediately got down to business was the ultimate tribute to our culture of 'one for all, all for one, but team above all'.

Ravi has been a towering presence all these years, a tremendous influence whose stature allows him to speak his mind and to treat the established and the rookie with the same amount of equanimity. If you have any doubts, perhaps this will help you make up your mind.

We had comfortably won the first of three One Day Internationals (ODIs) in Nottingham on the tour of England in 2018, and reached Lord's aiming to sew up the series. Fielding first, we allowed the game to drift a little towards the end, and England posted 322, with Joe Root scoring a century and David Willey taking us to the cleaners at the death. We knew we hadn't had a great outing with the ball or in the field, but we also knew that we were capable of chasing the total down. After all, we had won the first game by eight wickets with 59 balls to spare when our target was 269.

We were in the hunt when Virat and Suresh Raina were batting, but as we lost wickets, MS was left with only the bowlers for company going into the last 10 overs. Uncharacteristically, he shut shop, and even though our required rate in the last 10 was nearly 13 an over, we only managed some 20 runs in the next six overs. That was the innings when MS got to 10,000 ODI runs—a very significant milestone. We were all thrilled for him, but we also wanted to know why he hadn't made even a token attempt at the target.

Ravi, meanwhile, was seething. He was furious not because we lost by 86 runs, but how we lost the game, how we went down without putting up a fight. We didn't go for the target, we didn't go down throwing a punch, we just went down tamely. The head coach wasn't going to let that one sail harmlessly by.

The decider was in Headingley, and we had a team meeting the previous day. The entire squad was in attendance, including all members of the support staff, and I knew Ravi was going to make a strong point. He was at his loudest and fiercest as he said, 'No matter who you may be, there should not be another occasion when we lose a match not trying to win it. It will not happen under my watch. And if anyone does it, that will be the last bloody game of cricket they will play under my watch. You can lose a cricket game, no shame in that, but you will not lose like this.'

MS was sitting right there in the front, and while Ravi's words were meant for the team, his eyes were trained on MS. To the former skipper's great credit, he didn't flinch, he never broke eye contact with Ravi. He didn't look here and there or fidget because one of his many admirable qualities is his ability to take the knocks, especially when he knows in his heart of hearts that he deserves them.

That was hard for all of us to be a part of. I can't think of too many other coaches who would have done what Ravi did. I mean, we are talking M.S. Dhoni, Superman. He has won so many games for the country. All the youngsters listening to that felt, 'Wow, he is doing that to M.S. Dhoni'. So, the message was clear to everyone: you have to do your best to win games for the country. This is the brand of cricket we want to play and this is how we don't want to play. Again, that's suggestive of what we have done with this team. The team culture allowed Ravi and MS to live and work in synergy despite what had happened.

It's this same determination to play our own brand of cricket that drove us to take the unusual decision—not to us but for the thousands who felt otherwise at the time—to bat first in the Johannesburg Test in 2018. Perhaps, conventional wisdom dictated that on a surface of that nature, we should field first if we won the toss. After healthy debates in the dressing room, we decided that even though the series had already been lost, our best chance of winning lay in batting first and putting runs on the board.

I must admit there was a little bit of ego in that call, a little bit of our pride being stung after we failed to convert promising situations into victories in the first two Tests when we fell short chasing totals, but a significant influencer in that call was our game plan and the reading of the conditions. We didn't expect anything different than the track we got in Cape Town for the first Test, where we should have won but didn't, or in Johannesburg for the last game—a surface that had 'dangerous' written all over it.

South Africa, we assumed correctly, were desperate for revenge after what happened in India in 2015, when we beat them 3-0 on turning tracks. We knew they would prepare pitches to suit their strength, and we were fine with it because by then, we had started to approach every match, no matter where we played, as a home Test. We were taken aback, I must admit, at how under- (or over, depending on how you look at it) prepared the Wanderers strip looked, but we were not too fazed, to be honest.

It was a terrific Test to win, a result that was a direct consequence of our by-now well-entrenched culture of playing to win, not taking a backward step, wanting to play fearless cricket. We didn't want to bowl first as a defensive move. Old demons were being recalled, we were being dismissed as bad travellers and there was a lot of pride in the way we wanted to travel. We knew we were not as bad as we were playing.

We wanted to bat first, get runs on the board and put South Africa under pressure. We felt the pitch would only worsen as the game progressed. There was no way of it getting better at any stage, so our best chance of winning was to bat first. We played Pandya, which again gave us five bowling options, and while we didn't put too many on the board in the first innings, we were comfortable with our tally of 187.

A top bowling effort, with Jasprit Bumrah and Bhuvneshwar Kumar (Bhuvi) leading the charge, kept South Africa down to 194, and we hustled and scrapped and battled to 247, leaving us to defend 241 on the third and fourth days. The game was halted late on day three when Dean Elgar ducked into a not-so-short ball. Surprisingly, when the covers were removed the next morning, there was a thin layer of water on the pitch. Somehow, due to overnight and early morning rains, water seemed to have made its way onto the surface despite the protection. It was quite unbelievable! Not only did the game start an hour late, the pitch became damp, settled down and got a lot slower.

With this unexpected bonus, Elgar and Hashim Amla built a terrific partnership, I have to acknowledge, but I was more taken aback by the discipline with which the fast bowlers bowled. It was the first time we were playing without a spinner. We were literally showing off our fast bowling armoury, and they responded brilliantly on the fourth morning by not conceding too many runs at all in the first session. We knew that as the day went on, the pitch would dry up. We needed 40 runs to play with when the second new ball was due, no matter how many wickets South Africa had in hand.

As it turned out, Ishant Sharma dismissed Hashim just before the new ball could be taken, courtesy a superb catch at mid-wicket by Hardik. At the time, South Africa needed 117 more with eight wickets standing, and Hashim's fall opened the doors as we bulldozed through the order. We had Bumrah, Bhuvi, Ishant, Mohammed Shami and Hardik, and each of them was impeccable. South Africa were blown away by our fast men, the last nine wickets keeling over for just 53. It was a great victory.

Bhuvi was the Player of the Match for his all-round exploits as he vindicated our call to leave him out of the second Test in Centurion, even though he had picked up a five-for in Cape Town. We have been strong advocates and practitioners of the horses-for-courses philosophy, and felt in our collective wisdom that Bhuvi's style of bowling wouldn't have been ideal in Centurion, where we were confronted with a white deck, a *paata,* as we call it in India. We needed someone who could hit the deck as a fast bowler. That was one factor. The other was that we knew Bhuvi's body. He is not someone who could give you three back-to-back Tests with the same intensity because his body is like that. You need to use players based on their strength. If we needed Bhuvi to be at his best for Johannesburg, we had to rest him in Centurion. There was a week between the second and third Tests, so Bhuvi would get 12 days during which he could train away from the game to keep his bowling intact and come to Johannesburg a better bowler rather than a tired bowler. It might seem too obvious to necessitate stating, but these decisions were largely arrived at after talking to the player concerned, not thrust on the individual as seems to be the perception in some quarters.

I am sure Indian teams of the past approached Test cricket

with a must-win mentality too, but I can't second-guess their discussions and game plans. What I can say is that from 2015, we embarked on a journey of rediscovery that has occasionally been frustrating but primarily rewarding and fulfilling. If the processes being diligently put in place and yielding the desired results doesn't delight you as a player or a coach, then rest assured, nothing else will.

3

CRACKING THE
COMMUNICATION CODE

'Watch the fun from the other end till you get your breath back.'

Communication is a double-edged sword. It is a necessary tool for the exchange of views, ideas and information, of course, but it needs to be used judiciously so that it doesn't backfire. Sometimes, just saying the right things alone might not be enough. A lot depends on when and how the message is being passed across.

Like most important things in life, there is no set template when it comes to communication. As a coach, you need to work out what's the language best suited to each individual—who can understand jargons, who needs things to be broken down into everyday examples. I am a firm believer that less is more, that overloading a player with information doesn't always produce the desired results. I also encourage players to learn on their own by nudging them in the right direction because if you empower them, the learnings will be permanent, whereas if you spoon-feed them, the message will be forgotten in the immediacy of its effectiveness or otherwise.

As far as the coaching group is concerned, one of the

non-negotiables is being honest about developing a culture where you can look each player in the eye and tell him the truth, no matter how bitter or unpalatable that might be. Agreed, we lost the final of the WTC, but in the last six to seven years (2015 onwards), the Indian team has spoken in a particular language to its fans, thanks to the brand of cricket they have portrayed, and that too is a kind of communication of intent.

It perhaps should not be so, but when it comes to the support staff, one of the important aspects of communication is what kind of vibes we give out to the players. Sometimes, as coaches, we are under pressure, we feel the desperate need to uptick the 'Win' column. While there is a lot of talk about the processes and not worrying too much about the outcome in the short term, the urge to stack up wins can become pressing if a few results haven't gone your way. In times like that, it is very easy to unwittingly transmit negative vibes or negative energy. During those rough phases, it's essential to try and keep a poker face, without going into your shell. Only we know what each one of us is going through. In that sense, we are like a duck on water—very calm and composed when you look at what's visible, but with the legs flapping wildly and frantically beneath the surface.

Sometimes, no matter how honest and well-intentioned you might be, if the coach reveals his nervousness of wanting the team to do well, it might impact the team negatively. If you are open about your frustrations and observations, no matter how valid they might be, it could end up sending the wrong message. Maybe members of the support staff or the reserves sitting on the outside could spread the word. A coach has to be very wary; he should say the right things and not necessarily the correct things, if you get what I mean. His words should create the right atmosphere for the team to thrive and flourish because ultimately, that is the endeavour of the entire contingent.

You have to always be very careful with what you say even

when you think no one is watching or listening. There are several instances where, irrespective of what is happening around you, you are better off simply keeping your silence and watching the match as if you are as detached from it as possible. That's very difficult, in fact almost impossible to do, but it's an art we must learn if we are to be an effective coach.

Basically, like batting, it all boils down to timing. Yes, giving the correct inputs is very important, but many a time, you must wait for the right opportunity, when the player is open to feedback. When a player is closed, even if you say the right things, he can take it the wrong way, which can then cause much turmoil in his mind, leading to the team not being in the best space.

I alluded earlier to complete and total honesty within the team set-up, and that has been a constant over my seven years with the team (2014–21), when Duncan, Anil Kumble and Ravi were the coaches. Messages were transmitted from one source to another in a pleasant, seamless manner. Take the Test series against Australia at home in 2017, for instance, when Anil was the head coach. We had lost the first Test in Pune by a wide margin and were under the pump in the next game in Bengaluru. We were bowled out for 189 on day one and Australia had got off to an excellent start, 40 without loss, with David Warner looking in ominously good touch.

As we were headed for our rooms that evening, Ashwin suddenly got this idea of going over the stumps to Warner to exploit the rough outside his leg stump and bowl him round his legs. Ashwin's theory was sound—even if he didn't manage to immediately get Warner out, that line of attack would serve the additional purpose of stopping the score board from moving rapidly. At the time, Warner was a very explosive player. He was threatening to take the game away from us. All Ashwin wanted was to target the rough, dry up the runs and hopefully get one to turn sharply to bowl Warner behind his legs or across his body. He wanted to use the same spots from where Lyon had got the ball to turn on day one. Ashwin felt that while the ball was turning from outside off stump to the right-handed batter (or from outside leg to a left-hander like Warner), nothing was happening from the middle of the surface, when it was pitched on the stump line.

After giving it much thought, Ashwin darted across to Virat's room in the night for a frank discussion on his plans and why he thought they would work. Convinced about Ashwin's line of reasoning, Virat engaged his ace off-spinner in a long conversation. They went to the drawing board, worked out the field according to their plans and executed those plans to perfection the following morning. Almost magically, Warner was dismissed by a ball that pitched outside leg and spun across him. He tried to pad the ball away but was defeated by the sharp turn, and though he tried to follow the ball with his hands, it did enough to curl away from him and hit the off stump. That was a great example of the kind of communication processes we had facilitated within the group, encouraging players to speak to us or to each other freely and without inhibitions. When something like this comes off, there is a great deal of satisfaction at not just the coming to fruition of smart planning and perfect implementation but also at the success of a process we had striven diligently to put in place.

Equally satisfying, if not more, was what happened on the final day of the Sydney Test in January 2021. We needed to bat out more than 45 overs when Ashwin joined Vihari in the middle at the fall of the fifth wicket. Jadeja was injured and would only bat if desperately needed to do so, and only the pacers were left otherwise, so in effect, this pair was our best and perhaps last bet to salvage a draw.

When we arrived at the Sydney Cricket Ground on the final morning, we were two down with 98 overs to negotiate. (Rohit and Shubman were dismissed the previous evening.) Soon, as we entered the dressing room, one of the locals looking after our requirements bustled across and asked us if we wanted the lunch served at the ground itself, or if we'd rather they sent it across to our hotel. His not-so-subtle message was that we wouldn't last till lunch! I laughed at that well-placed salvo, which was typical Australian, typical of how they come at you.

Anyway, we were still afloat at lunch, thanks to Pujara and Rishabh. After a grand partnership of 148 that threatened to turn the match on its head, they both got out within 25 runs of each other, leaving Vihari and Ashwin holding the baby. I could sense the tension and nervousness in the very small dressing room at the Sydney Cricket Ground. If we lost the game, we could kiss our chances of making the WTC final goodbye. We could forget about thinking of another series win in Australia.

But, sitting beside each other, the members of the support staff told one another that we would not let anyone know how we were feeling. 'Let's keep encouraging these two guys every ball, no matter what happens,' was our mantra. Ravi bought into the idea, and believe you me, for the duration of that partnership—nearly 260 deliveries—he would scream his lungs out after every ball, screaming 'shabash' loudly enough each time for all 15 gentlemen in the middle to hear clearly. If the situation weren't so dire, it would have been hilarious.

Vihari and Ashwin came in at tea, and while we converged to congratulate and encourage them, a tactical call was also made. Vihari had pulled his hamstring and was not able to play Lyon convincingly because his movements were restricted. He couldn't put in the good, long stride. Ashwin, meanwhile, was being subjected to a bouncer barrage from the quicks. So, it was decided that Ashwin, at home against Lyon, would take on the off-spinner and Vihari would negotiate the three-pronged pace attack.

After having stuck to their respective ends of the bargain, for some strange reason, they took a single, which exposed Vihari to

Lyon and Ashwin to the fast men. A couple of singles later, the situation was unaltered and Ravi was starting to lose his shirt. He summoned substitute Shardul Thakur and told him, 'Listen to me very carefully, and repeat this to them: No matter what happens, Vihari will handle the fast bowlers, Ashwin will play Lyon. No singles, no change of ends, period. Got it?'

Shardul smiled coyly and said, 'Yes, sir', and charged to the middle with a bottle of water for Ashwin.

After exchanging a few words with the two batters, he ran back in. 'Did you pass on my message?' Ravi growled. 'Yes, sir, of course,' Shardul replied.

It was only much, much later, after we had pulled the fat out of the fire and escaped with one of the greatest draws, that the real story came out. It seems when Shardul went in, Ashwin asked him what was being said in the dressing room. Shardul replied, 'They are saying many things, but you guys don't worry. You are batting well, just continue doing the same things.' He didn't pass on Ravi's message; instead, he told the batters exactly what they wanted to hear at that time. Perhaps he sized up that passing on the instructions, however steeped in logic they might be, could disrupt the flow of the batters and the zone they were in, so he passed on a message he thought was the best under the circumstances. Hats off to him! In a direct way, that is linked to the kind of empowerment we gave the players, and which they learnt to use judiciously.

Staying on the topic of player empowerment, I would like to recall what happened in Canberra on the 2020–21 tour of Australia, during the first Twenty20 International. We had conceded the ODI series, even though we won the last game, and were determined to get off to a good start to the 20-over showdown before the Test series.

We were looking for a strong finish to the innings, with Mitchell Starc bowling the last over. Off the second delivery, a screamer at around 146 kmph, Jadeja was dropped at point. The ball had gone off the top edge onto his helmet, but Jaddu recovered from that blow to smash two boundaries subsequently. By then, though, he had already strained his hamstring.

I was in the dugout, ready to set up fielding stations immediately at the end of the innings before Australia could begin their chase. Seated by my side were Sanju Samson and Mayank Agarwal. Suddenly, Sanju piped up, 'Sir, the ball hit Jaddu's helmet, didn't it? Why can't we seek a concussion replacement? We can get another bowler in instead of Jaddu.'

That is where I saw a captain in that youngster. I urged him to dash across to Ravi and convey his sentiments, and Ravi, too, saw merit in Sanju's thinking. In any case, the concussion rules allowed us to make a change if a player was hit on the head, so when Jadeja came off the field, Ravi told him, 'Well played, now go to the dressing room, hold an ice-pack to your head and sit down quietly.'

After the doctor examined Jadeja, Ravi walked up to match referee David Boon and requisitioned Yuzvendra Chahal as the concussion sub. The doctor who assessed Jadeja said if he felt even slightly giddy, he must not take the field. As Boon approved our request for a concussion sub, you could see that Justin Langer was losing his shirt. The Australian coach knew Chahal would be a big threat given that the surface was assisting the spinners, and from his obvious displeasure, you could make out that psychologically, Australia were rattled.

It was impossible for the team not to be affected by their coach's open show of anger and annoyance. Mentally, they were down even before the start of their chase, and it was no surprise that Chahal tied them up in knots, finishing with three for 25 and being named the Player of the Match. To cap off the fairy tale, Sanju took a brilliant catch running in from deep mid-wicket to get rid of Steve Smith.

Sanju's quick thinking that led to Chahal's induction is an incident that will stay with me for life. That's where you saw a captain in Sanju, you saw a leader who was thinking about the game. He was not thinking about how he got out, he was thinking for the team. These are the moments that reveal one's character. This was a classic case of reverse learning. Neither Ravi nor Virat thought of this scenario; Sanju summed things up in a jiffy and wasn't afraid to communicate his thoughts. That's a big tick as far as I am concerned.

Ravi is a fabulous communicator who talks straight and doesn't mince words, whether you are an established superstar or a newbie. He is the one who passes on the tough messages—calls pertaining to being dropped from the XI to the players concerned. There was a time in 2016 when Virat was very eager to be the captain of the white-ball team too. He said a few things that showed he was looking for the captaincy. One evening, Ravi called him and said, 'Look, Virat, MS gave it [the captaincy] to you in red-ball cricket. You have to respect him. He will give it to you in limited-overs cricket, too, when the time is right. Unless you respect him now, tomorrow when you are the captain, you won't get the respect from your team. Respect him now, irrespective of what is going on. It will come to you, you don't have to run behind it.' To his credit, Virat took the advice on board. Eventually, in a year's time, he got the white-ball captaincy too.

Ravi's stature helps him communicate the 'harsh' decisions to the players effortlessly. He has been in cricket for more than 40 years—playing, broadcasting, watching and coaching. That really helps, especially in Indian cricket. He is not afraid of reading the riot act, which you can do only if you don't have an agenda. It is only when, as a coaching unit, you have an agenda with a player or with some of the administrators, that all these things become a challenge. That, or when you want to hold onto your place, in which case, you can never be an effective coach. That's something Ravi, or anybody else in our coaching group, has never done; we were never greedy, we didn't want to hold onto our positions. Every year was a bonus, but we had to do our job with absolute honesty, look the player in the eye, tell him what we had to. All the support staff was one unit. If the players see that the support staff aren't united, they might play you against each other and the situation becomes a little different.

The support staff respected Ravi and he knew everything that was going on in the team. The younger players confided in me or the trainer or someone else because we were easier to relate to. They didn't approach Ravi because of the age difference, perhaps. But he got all information. You can't see all this from the outside, but this is a well-oiled machine. If everyone knows their roles and does their jobs correctly, then the language the team speaks on the field is different. The kind of cricket you want to play, the brand of cricket, that's a language on its own.

When we played England at home in our last series of the WTC league, we knew we had to win 2-1 or better to make it to the final. We had bounced back from the loss of the first Test in Chennai to win the next two games but were in a huge hole in the last Test in Ahmedabad. Even though we had bowled England out for 205 on the first day, we stumbled to 153 for six by tea on the second day. A draw was out of the question, and if we lost the match, the series would be squared 2-2, which meant we wouldn't qualify for the final.

Rishabh and Washi were practically our last hope. Fortunately, because there was an extra spinner, Axar Patel, the tail was slightly better. But still, we were well behind the eight-ball. Rishabh and Washi came in at tea, the former huffing and puffing as he told Ravi, 'Sir, so many steps to climb, it's more tiring than batting in the middle.' We could all relate to what he was saying, there were 91 steps between the ground and the dressing room!

As the squad burst out into laughter, Ravi signalled to the two batters to join him. 'The WTC final is looking far away now, but I don't care about that,' he told them. 'I want you to go out there and enjoy your batting. You are batting in India, their spinners are bowling, they should be scared to bowl to you, it should not be the other way round. Just enjoy your batting. You have had a good look by now. Just forget the result. If the series is drawn 2-2, I don't care. Just forget about everything else and have fun. We have played well right throughout the season. Under tough circumstances after Covid-19, we had six good months of Test cricket, that's enough. Don't worry about the consequences, go out there and enjoy yourselves.' These were the exact words they needed to hear. Straightaway, he took the pressure off the two youngsters

Whether Ravi said it to mask the pressure he was under or he genuinely meant it is a different thing; he said what he thought was appropriate for the occasion. Sometimes, even though you want to say something, you end up saying something very different to the player. You have to affirm what he wants to hear because there is a difference in their perspective and ours. As coaches, we have to be careful; from time to time, we need to resort to fabrication of encouragement and fake smiles when things are not going well. That is a must to keep the space healthy and pleasant. We just can't be overtly critical because we often tend to take things too seriously.

Of course, everyone knows what happened after tea. Rishabh smashed the bowlers around as he scored his first 100 in India. Washi just missed out on his century. Axar weighed in with the bat and we opened up a massive lead. The innings win and a slot in the final followed naturally.

As a fielding coach, my biggest learning in communication

has been timing. Even though you may have the right things to say, when you say it is very important. You must talk to a player when he is open and receptive. Some of the best coaching advice I have given have not been in a cricket setting. It could be in a coffee shop or an airport lounge, and not necessarily about fielding. It could be about a player making a minor technical tweak or changing his mindset. The best messages are passed on in these situations. Off the field is when the player is most relaxed, more open and actually listening to you. Sometimes on the field, during the heat of battle, the player wouldn't be listening or won't be thinking about it enough to implement it.

During the 2019 World Cup, K.L. Rahul moved up from the middle order to partner Rohit once Shikhar got injured after the Australia game. KL had a decent run, though many people pointed a finger at his strike rate. I knew he was a little light on confidence, especially after being dismissed for a duck against England in Birmingham, caught and bowled by Chris Woakes. I was aware that dismissal troubled him no end.

Our next game was also in Birmingham, against Bangladesh. There's always been a strong comfort level between KL and me as I have seen him from his Under-16 days. I took him out to a nice organic coffee shop, which we both frequented, merely to get him away from his room and to stop him from moping, if that was what he was doing.

We had just settled into our seats when KL started to speak—about his batting, his mindset, about how he had got out to Woakes, trying to play the flick and being caught and bowled off the leading edge. It did look ungainly for a batter of his class, but I bit my tongue. This was about KL, about him wanting to talk and vent. I would only talk if he specifically asked a question, and even then, I wouldn't reply so much as guide him to the right answers.

Another important aspect of communication is that the

answers come from the player, that you become the listener. You listen with intent and genuine interest without thinking about what you want to say next. When you are listening, you are not thinking about your next repartee. That's how that vibe goes, they open up and talk.

I gave him neither technical nor tactical inputs. When I did speak, I tried to provide him with the comfort he was seeking without actually asking. I reinforced his credentials, reminded him of his strengths and his role. I told him that considering Rohit's form, all he had to do was give Rohit the strike initially and understand how well his own hands and feet were working that day. 'Watch the fun from the other end till you get your breath back,' I suggested. Obviously, when you first go in, you will be breathing hard because you want to get runs every single innings, and especially when it's a World Cup.

When we left an hour later, it looked as if a load had been lifted off his shoulders. He made a fine 70-odd against Bangladesh and then scored a 100 against Sri Lanka. I am not saying he got runs because of that conversation we had, but it was very satisfying as a coach to believe you had played a small part in freeing up his mind, more than anything else. If I were given to hype, I'd say it was one of the best coffees I've had!

■

As coaches, we need our release too. It's humanly impossible to put on a brave and positive face all the time and not be affected by what's going on around us. Our release is in talking to each other. As I have said, we have a terrific relationship. Arun and I have been coaching together right from our Under-19 stints. When you coach Under-19 teams, you know how teenagers are. They make a mistake out of nowhere, that's just the way they are wired. The game will be going well and suddenly they will make a series of errors and in no time you lose the game, when least expected. You think you are cruising and within minutes, the game turns on its head and you end up losing it. So, when you are coaching in Under-19 cricket, you realize a mistake is round the corner. You know nothing is over till it is actually over. Whether you are winning or losing, things can change drastically in a matter of 15 minutes.

We got so used to coaching Under-19 kids, it got a little easier coming up and coaching the senior team because that ebb and flow was not there. Yes, matches changed path or direction, but it was more controllable. When I felt frustrated, my release was going and chatting with Arun. We always had very honest discussions. Even with Ravi, in the evenings, we would have a glass of wine or sip a beer, talk about what happened. Whatever we spoke was within the four walls. We sorted out the plans for the next day. We got stuff off our chest. We had this close group where we could take the pressure off each other.

I often use the 2012 Under-19 World Cup final as a reference point, when Arun and I had travelled as coaches of Unmukt Chand's team. At the time, the final was the be-all and end-all of our lives. Winning the Under-19 World Cup would be a big stamp on our CV, especially because we were aspiring to at some point be a part of the coaching staff of the Indian cricket team.

Things went according to plan in the first half of the final when we stuck Australia in and restricted them to 225. Our reply received an early jolt, but then Unmukt and Baba Aparajith steadied the ship and at 75 for one, we were well placed to go all the way. Not unexpectedly, we lost a few quick wickets, including that of Vihari. We were in a spot at 82 for three, with Akshdeep Nath slated to go in next, at No. 6. I watched him closely and could make out that he was very nervous. He was sweating profusely, his palms too were sweating—the situation had got to him. I quietly walked up to Arun and said, 'Paaji, there's a good chance he won't last long in his current state of mind, let's change things up and send Smit Patel at No. 6.'

Now, Smit was what you would call a 'bindaas' guy. The wicketkeeper-batter was having a good tournament. More importantly, he seemed quite relaxed and was the sort of player who didn't get overwhelmed by pressure. He also was a good student of the game, and so when Vijay Zol was dismissed on 97, we sent Smit ahead of Akshdeep.

I could barely watch the next passage of play. I would have given anything to slip into a sound sleep for two hours. That's what happens when you get so attached to and involved in the game, when you want the victory so desperately. At the time, I felt my coaching career depended on what unfolded over those two hours, even though I had no control over the events in the middle. Actually, that's the best feeling as a coach. That's why you do it, it is an addiction. You want that tension, you want that period of play where even though you are desirous of doing so much, all you can do is sit and watch helplessly, if impassively. A coach's true nature comes out during these phases, that is when you have to be at your best. That brings out how you want to communicate, how you want your team to be, what is the message you are sending out to the team. As a coach, you want to be in those situations where you know you can't do anything because you are outside the boundary line, but you can actually help by doing nothing. In this instance, we found the pot of gold at the end of the rainbow as Unmukt and Smit put on 130 and steered us to the title. I wish that was an everyday occurrence.

One of the golden rules in coaching is that less is more, that there is addition by subtraction. Especially during big events, the players are already motivated. They have done everything they could in the lead-up to the competition, they are all geared up. You must take a back seat and watch things happen. As part of the communication process, it is very important to know when to butt in and say something, and when not to. Most of the time, we are dealing with elite cricketers, so less is definitely more. That doesn't mean you don't say anything at all or that you don't do any homework. You watch videos, you make your notes, you do whatever you have to, but addition by subtraction has worked very well for me over the last seven years. Sometimes, you feel the need to talk, but too many instructions can queer the pitch, put a spoke in the wheel.

Communication is a weapon you must use carefully. When you talk too much, you end up making mistakes. That is something I have learnt. It is an important tool, but it can easily get misconstrued or misused. You can end up sending the wrong message. The key is knowing what the player wants to hear. Having played the game a little bit, you as a player know that in a particular situation, if you go to a coach, this is what you want to hear. At tea, when a player walks in, you put yourself in his shoes. That makes things a lot clearer.

But you must strike a balance between what he wants to hear and what he needs to hear. If at all there is confusion in my mind or if I am not sure about something, then I don't say anything. My style of communication, especially with this team, has been asking questions and getting the answers from them rather than me giving the solutions. Basically, if the ball is not bouncing much, you ask a slip fielder, 'You are having to stand a little closer to the stumps than normal. Are you comfortable with that? Is there any part that's uncomfortable? Is there another way to do it?' That makes the player think; you are nudging them towards thinking instead of telling them what they should do. Even if it is not in his mind, I am nudging him in that direction. Like saying, 'Do I have to stay really low because there isn't much bounce?' I am not actually telling him anything.

That doesn't mean, of course, that everything takes a seamless hue. When Ravi came on as team director in England in late

2014, Arun, Sanjay and I, too, joined the team. Ahead of the 2015 World Cup, Ravi changed the way team meetings were run. Duncan's style involved putting up presentation slides, talking about them (he was the only one who spoke) and then everyone dispersing. MS hardly spoke as a rule, and in any case, he and Duncan would have had a chat before the team meeting.

Ahead of the World Cup, Ravi decided that the players would speak at the team meetings. That at every meeting, one by one, the batters would speak of their game plans, how they would approach different situations, what their plans are for each bowler in the opposition. After that, all-rounders Ashwin and Jadeja would hold forth, and at the end, the fast bowlers would express their thoughts. It was a very good system, I felt, because ultimately it was the players who had to perform out in the middle.

We had a similar exercise the day before the game against South Africa at the Melbourne Cricket Ground. That evening, I was at my old friend Noel Carr's place in Melbourne for dinner when I got a call from Arun, asking for my views on this new introduction. I knew I could speak freely to Arun, so I told him, 'It's a great concept, but we should be careful how often we do it. It's a golden goose, we should not kill it. If we do this before every game, its effectiveness will diminish. I feel it's better if we have such sessions before key matches.'

I didn't know, of course, that I was on speaker phone, that Ravi was listening in. I was fairly new to international cricket, and Ravi and I didn't really know each other all that well. Apparently he wasn't very amused by what he heard. 'Baadi,' he thundered, referring to Arun by his nickname, 'I told you these young coaches have no idea what I am doing. I had told you at the very beginning not to recommend such novice coaches.'

I was rattled. I knew there was merit in what I had told Arun, but I was unnerved by Ravi's reaction and didn't sleep very well that night. The next day, we turned in a brilliant performance in the field, we out-fielded South Africa for the first time. David Miller was run out, A.B. de Villiers was run out, thanks to great efforts by the fast bowlers, and we took all our catches. Ravi turned to me in the dressing room and said, 'Sri, great job. The way you have worked on the fielders is awesome.' I was mighty relieved. He had completely shed his ire of the previous night. And although he had been angry at the time, he did take my suggestion on board. Only when he felt each one had to know the others' game plan before a big game did he have inclusive, extended meetings thereafter.

Most of the good moments have been when the players found answers themselves, not being spoon-fed. In such cases, they understand that the ownership of decision-making is theirs and so there is a greater sense of responsibility. That's an effective way of communication, asking questions and nudging them towards finding their own solutions. That's empowerment. A good coach looks to empower his players rather than give solutions, which they will forget at the end of the day's play. If you steer them to find their own solutions, that is a permanent learning. It's a learning they will never forget. In a nutshell, that is the secret to good communication when it comes to a coach or a teacher.

4

THE FIELDING REVOLUTION

'If you don't mind, Sridhar sir, why should I listen to
you and follow the fielding drills you suggest?'

Sometime in 2018–19, Sunil Gavaskar told me, 'Sri, this is the second-best Indian fielding team in my involvement with the sport.'

I was curious to know which side he rated the best, but I couldn't quite muster up the courage to ask him, so I merely smiled and replied, 'Thank you, Sunny bhai.'

With his trademark mischievous smile, he asked, 'You don't want to know which was the best?' Without waiting for my reply, he continued, 'The team of the 1980s. That was a better fielding unit than this, and I am not joking. Look at the guys we had. Mohammad Azharuddin had just come in in the mid-1980s. We had Sadanand Viswanath behind the stumps. There was young blood in the form of Laxman Sivaramakrishnan and Chetan Sharma, and then we had Kapil Dev, Roger Binny and Madan Lal. It was a top fielding unit, very consistent. The way Azhar used to cover the boundaries, the way he used the angles, was excellent. And Kapil's throws were something else.'

As Sunny bhai walked away and I reflected on what he had

said, the phrase that stuck with me was 'very consistent'. The 1980s was a great fielding team because the difference between their good days and their bad days was miniscule. If on a good day, the team's productivity rating is 99 per cent, then on a bad day, you should be 96 per cent. It shouldn't be that you are 99 per cent on your returns on a good day and 80 per cent on a bad day. That, to me, is not a good fielding team, and that is what we drove into the Indian team during my seven-year stint.

It was after the advent of live television and white-ball cricket in the 1970s that fielding started to assume a certain significance worldwide. Until then, it was considered, at best, a necessary evil. The general perception was that there were only two skills in cricket—batting and bowling. We all knew Eknath Solkar was a great catcher and Sir Garfield 'Garry' Sobers was brilliant in the field, but there was limited to no footage. When Kerry Packer arrived with his World Series Cricket, players started to view fielding as a third skill. No longer were fielders clapping a good shot and fetching the ball from the boundary. They started to chase the ball, a little bit of effort was being made.

In my opinion, the 1990s brought a fourth skill into cricket— fitness, which changed the entire dynamics of the sport. South Africa and Bob Woolmer, their coach, were the first to hire strength and conditioning coaches on their return to international cricket in 1991. South Africa were unbelievable at the time, and much of it was to do with how much fitter their players were compared to the rest of the field. That opened everyone's eyes to the significance of fitness, and our great sport has never been the same again.

The last push India required in our quest to become a consistent global superpower came in the form of the IPL. Fitness was revolutionized, along with a lot of other things. The BCCI started investing heavily at the grassroots level. There were better grounds for our kids to start diving without the fear of getting injured. The IPL became the best coach, television became the best coach, in my opinion. Kids learn more from watching television these days than they do from a coach, as far-fetched as that might seem.

Of course, the putting in motion of plans will take time to fructify. The IPL started in 2008, and with the BCCI ploughing the money back into improving infrastructure in Tier 2 and Tier 3 cities, you could see the transformation unfolding before your eyes. In five years, since the commencement of the IPL, India would vie for the title of the best fielding team in the world.

■

It was during the 2008–09 season that the fielding framework was established at the NCA. Robin Singh was travelling with the national side as the fielding coach, and the BCCI felt the need to have a full-fledged coach at the academy as well. I believe the addition of the first full-time head of the fielding unit at the NCA was a step in the right direction, and not because I was the one appointed to that position. And once the IPL started, there was a huge mental shift, a paradigm shift in the way young players looked at fielding.

Before that, India were consistent without being outstanding. The 2003 World Cup unit was a top-class fielding side. India were passable in 2007. If you take the 2011 World Cup, it was such an experienced team. I was supposed to go to Anantapur in Andhra Pradesh for a women's camp when Gary Kirsten approached me, asking me if I could assist the World Cup team during their three-week preparatory camp in Bengaluru. It was too big an opportunity for me to pass up the Indian coach's offer.

Although that was an unbelievable team, it was as if they left fielding almost to choice—the choice of the player concerned.

It's not that they never used to work on their fielding, but it wasn't their top priority by any stretch of the imagination. I used to set up all these stations at the M. Chinnaswamy Stadium, the nets were outside the main stadium, at the NCA. The lone guy who used to turn up consistently every day for fielding was Ashwin, sometimes accompanied by S. Sreesanth. Only on a couple of days did we have team fielding sessions, where we split the squad into three different groups and did some drills. Other than that, although they held their own and especially in the final against Sri Lanka, that team was a World Cup winner purely on experience. That's my assessment only so far as fielding is concerned. They knew what they were capable of physically, they knew they couldn't turn up every day and have half-hour fielding sessions. They were aware their bodies couldn't take that workload leading into the World Cup. And they also knew that they could turn it on when needed. This team was an exception to the rule of thumb based purely on the collective experience among them as a unit.

Even a year before we came on board in 2014, India had a top fielding side at the 2013 International Cricket Council (ICC) Champions Trophy. It was a youthful team—Jadeja, a young Rohit, a young Virat. The way they fielded set a benchmark as to how good a white-ball fielding group India were. There was an opportunity there for us to become one of the most consistent fielding units in the world. India were easily the best fielding team in the tournament; we were a gun team. The fielders considered themselves an attacking tool rather than thinking they were just there to save runs. That was a huge mental shift.

The players knew everyone was watching on television. They knew they could create a piece of magic whenever the ball came to them. They were looking for opportunities—that was the kind of team culture. It's something that must have been spoken about by the management. There must have been a conscious effort to make this happen because they all had the skill sets. MS wasn't obsessed with the results, but he never compromised on effort on the field.

When I joined the team, one of the first things I asked the skipper was what he wanted of me; if there were specific areas he would like to see addressed. MS was on the massage table at the Marriott in Bristol, and I had carried a list with me of 25 players or so. I read out the names to him and he had some observation or the other about most of them. When I reached Ashwin's name, MS said, 'Can you work on his agility? I want him to be quick in changing directions. He has got good hands, good reaction skills, but if he can improve his agility, we can get more out of him as a fielder, especially in white-ball cricket.'

That became my immediate focus, with the 50-over World Cup a little over six months away. I knew I could never make an Ashwin into a Jadeja, but certainly, we could make Ashwin a better Ashwin, a better version of himself. Yes, he had his limitations, given his body type, but there was still scope for improvement and that's what we targeted.

I was only one of the cogs involved in that process. We sat with the trainer, the physio and the dietician. We brought about a change in his training programme. We tweaked his diet a little, shifting it to a high-protein one, which he was happy to follow. We started doing movement drills, and he concentrated more on power and strength exercises. Seven years on, Ashwin is a better fielder than he was in 2014, even though he hasn't gotten any younger. He is not a great sprinter; he has got limitations in terms of his acceleration. But once the ball is hit at him, he is more than just a safe fielder. He gets down a lot lower than he used to. The great thing about Ashwin is that he is an exceptionally good student of the game. Coaching him is a thrill because he is quick to understand what you're trying to say. If I tell him that he is not getting into a split position and so is a little late on the ball, he is quick to respond even if I have not shown him footage.

Being with Ashwin, I was struck by one of our early conversations, in my first week with the national team. Non-confrontationally, he asked me, 'If you don't mind, Sridhar sir, why should I listen to you and follow the fielding drills you suggest? Why should I do what you are asking me to? From 2011 to 2014, we had Trevor Penney as the fielding coach. Now you have come in, you will be there for let's say two to three years. You will say something; you will go away. Then a new fielding coach will come. If I am honest, in the next three years, I have a lot at stake. I should be convinced that what you are saying is going to work for me. It should help my game, otherwise why should I listen to you?' We knew each other quite well by then, and I immediately got where he was coming from. His questions set me thinking: how much should I coach? What is coaching really?

Yes, I had been with the Under-19 team. Yes, I had tasted great success with them—we won 11 of the 12 tournaments during that period; we won a World Cup; we won three Asia Cups. I worked with Kings XI Punjab in IPL 2014, the year we reached the final. I had a good rapport with the players. But the Indian team was a different cup of tea altogether. It was after that chat with Ashwin that I realized I had to tweak my style of functioning just a little bit. That I should be more of a facilitator than an enforcer. I worked hard to ensure that line didn't get blurred, and I'd like to believe that approach did bring the right results.

Now getting back to my early days with the Indian team. Following MS's inputs, we began to get our fielding house in order with the World Cup in mind. We were playing West Indies at the Feroz Shah Kotla in October 2014—a match we won comfortably but where we were absolutely shoddy on the field. MS was furious at what he perceived to be lack of effort and dipping fitness standards. In the dressing room, he ripped the team to shreds and gave them an ultimatum, making it clear that if they didn't meet certain standards in fielding and fitness, they wouldn't make the World Cup cut, no matter what name they answered to. That showed me the kind of fielding culture he was looking to establish in white-ball cricket.

That culture inevitably percolated to every level. Understandably, it's a lot easier at the junior grade to get youngsters to be at a good level of intensity for sustained periods because they are 18 to 19 years of age and are looking to take the next step forward. It does become a bit of a challenge at the senior level, when there is so much more at stake. But through sheer hard work and stubbornness, for a large part of 2015, we were an excellent fielding unit. Somehow, in the ICC tournaments, across players and generations, we have had the knack of turning it on in terms of on-field performances. In recent times, we have been more consistent in our displays in bilateral series too.

I learnt some harsh lessons reasonably early on in my stint with the Indian team. One of the most impactful ones came at the Kotla, in the final Test of the 2015 series against South Africa. We already enjoyed a winning 2-0 lead, and by tea on day five, it seemed as if South Africa might succeed in preventing us from scoring a third successive victory. With AB putting on a stonewalling act for the ages and receiving support from Hashim Amla and Faf du Plessis on a dead track, South Africa were only five down at the final interval of the series. We were going to give it one final push on a gloomy December evening, but we were also reconciled to a stalemate, if it came to that.

At tea time, we had a quick discussion on reverse swing. It was decided that Umesh Yadav would begin proceedings alongside Ashwin. We told Umesh to drop his bowling hand a little and deliver slightly away from his ear so that the change of angle of release, a more round-arm option, could help him find reverse. That's when I took my eye off the ball.

The team talk done with, I slipped into the common area between the teams and started chatting with Prasanna Agoram, the video analyst of the South African side and an old friend. I totally lost track of time. Normally, by the time the players get back on the field for the start of a session, I'd have set up a catching station; I'd be armed with a mitt in case somebody wanted to bowl a couple of warm-up deliveries. This evening, I forgot all that when suddenly I heard someone call out 'Sri bhai, Sri bhai' stridently.

I froze for a second when I heard the voice from the ground. I sneaked a peek at my watch and my heart sank. I sprinted down the copious steps to the ground, but by the time I was at ground level, the umpires had already walked in and the Indian team was following suit. Virat turned back and finally spotted me. His face was neutral, but he spread his arms wide and shrugged his shoulders. You didn't need to be an expert in body language to figure out what he was trying to convey.

The post-tea session was a brilliant passage of play. Umesh bowled superbly, Saha took a blinder leaping to his right, Ashwin got AB at backward short leg and the game just changed in a jiffy. But none of it registered. I was so dejected that I had failed in my duty. It was the last session of the series, and I had taken my eye off the ball. When the captain looked at me in disappointment, the first thought that occurred to me was that I must walk away from the Indian team, quit my job. I am glad I chose the more constructive option, of treating every day as my first day at the office, no matter what.

I further learnt how to look at each day as day one at work from D. Raghavendra, the tireless throwdown specialist. Even today, despite so many years with the team, he works like he has just come on board. He doesn't relax for even a second. He has managed to retain the same alacrity and intent as on his first day. That reinforced my commitment to not become complacent because the team would move on, irrespective of whether I was with them or not. That's why even when it drizzled, or when the end of a match was nigh, we, as support staff, set up the same drills as on the first day of the Test match. Experience had taught us that the day you didn't set up something, one player or the other would walk up saying he'd like to do a specific drill. That's why, for the last many years, we made it a point to be prepared. Whether the players turn up or not is their prerogative.

Small but hugely meaningful gestures make all this worth the while. We were in Kolkata for the second ODI against Australia in September 2017. Virat and I were sitting in a corner, fooling around with yellow balls we used for catching because they were a touch lighter and swung a little bit. Virat picked up a ball, wrote a few words and handed it over to me. It read: 'Sri bhai, thank you for always pushing us and allowing us to be at our best.' That signed ball occupies pride of place in my office room.

■

A great fielder is one who makes a difficult game look simple. That's why, to me, the most complete Indian fielder I have worked with is Suresh Raina. He was a great slip fielder, an outstanding outfield catcher, very good with direct hits and showed tremendous energy on the field. In that sense, he was the complete package. And that's also why I put Ricky Ponting and Andrew Symonds as the best fielders across the spectrum in my cricketing lifetime. Both were outstanding slip fielders, great in the circle. Symonds was stunning on the boundary line, covered ground exceptionally quickly and had a bullet throw. To me, he was the best all-time, all-round fielding package—direct hits from point, underarm hits and diving stops, and also awesome at short mid-wicket. I mean, I could go on and on.

Jadeja is another great fielder, though I wouldn't have him stand in the slip cordon. When I came in, Ashwin and Jadeja were slip fielders. I had a conversation with Duncan, asking him why Jadeja was standing at third slip and how much he had practised slip catching. Have you ever seen Jonty Rhodes in the slips? It's a specialized catching position, which requires special skills and loads of practise.

You will drop catches, make no mistake. One of my pet lines is, 'Show me one fielder who has not dropped a catch, I will show you God.' Simple. But the difference in output between your good day and bad day should be minimal. That was the endeavour throughout with this team. I remember the Champions Trophy in 2017, the league game against Pakistan. We fielded atrociously, dropped three catches and yet won the game by the proverbial country mile. In the next match against South Africa, we effected three run outs and held three brilliant catches. We won the match at The Oval on the back of our fielding; we bowled South Africa out for less than 200 and cruised home with 12 overs to spare.

We had a chat in the dressing room after the victory and I told the guys, 'Fantastic display today, but it should not be like this. It can't be that you field terribly one day and in the next game, you turn up as the best fielding team in the world. It's a good feeling today but ideally, there should not be this difference when you are ordinary one day and sublime the next. It's terrific that you lifted yourselves after the Pakistan game, but it's not fair. It shouldn't come to the point where you feel you have to win a game to stay afloat in a tournament or you have a point to prove, so you will go out there and put in your best effort. Whether you are No. 1 on the table or bringing up the rear, you have to be the same as far as fielding is concerned, you have to be consistent.'

So, to facilitate that process, we brought in consistency in having the right fielders at the same positions; having the right people at the right time at the right place. We transferred the responsibility to the fielder to think as a captain. You captain yourself; take the ego out. If you have to go to deep square-leg, go to deep square-leg. If you feel you are in a high-traffic zone, that the ball might come to you a lot and you are not confident, call another fielder to stand there. It's for the team; it's not about yourself. To convince them to embrace that responsibility takes time, like anything of this nature. But once they buy into it whole-heartedly, there is little that's more fulfilling.

Let's take Jadeja as an example. On the 2020–21 tour of Australia, he dropped a sitter in the second ODI in Sydney. As a team, we were having a bad time in the field, coming as we were after an unprecedented period of no activity, thanks to the lockdown. When Jadeja shelled a regulation catch at long-on, it was as if you had seen everything there was to on a cricket field. At the end of the game, he walked up, looked me in the eye and said, 'Sri bhai, sorry, I made a mess of it.' No excuses, no nothing. There were a few other boys with me at the time, and it was a good lesson for them. Whenever some of them made errors, they'd say the light was in the eye or the spike slipped, or any one of the myriad excuses we have all used. But Jadeja was honest in owning up his mistake.

Not only that, in the next game in Canberra, he took a screamer, running in from deep backward square and diving forward, to get rid of Cameron Green on the sweep. That's what top players do. When they screw up, they own it up. That is the first part of recovery and succeeding after a failure. After the Sydney miss, Jadeja didn't drop his body language. He went out the next game and made an excellent comeback after an ordinary performance by his own standards. There was a great aura of determination about him in his body language. That's what champions do. They handle setbacks brilliantly; they bounce back quickly and in style.

■

Yuzvendra Chahal broke into the Indian side in the middle of 2016. A little over a year later, he had taken giant strides towards becoming a permanent member of the limited-overs set-up, and by early 2018, we had clearly identified him and Kuldeep Yadav as crucial to our plans for the 50-over World Cup in England. Ravi told me to get them up to scratch. One (Kuldeep) was a very slow athlete; he didn't have any speed. The other was absolutely bones; he had nothing, no cushion in his palms. These two were proper work. Kuldeep, luckily, is a very hard worker. He put in the hard yards and never shied away from a practice session.

However, Chahal was a different kettle of fish. He had small hands and extremely thin fingers. Because he had had a few fractures on his fingers, he was justified in being a hesitant, wary catcher. He struggled to even form a proper cup in his hands because of the way his fingers were structured. He was a lot of work and given his body, it was very tough to subject him to a serious workload while also keeping him ready for the games.

In our final assignment before the World Cup, three T20Is and a five-match ODI showdown at home against Australia in February–March 2019, we decided that Chahal would be played sparingly. As it turned out, he only figured in three of those eight matches. We used those three weeks as a fielding camp for him. As much as the physical act of fielding, we were keen to work on his mindset. Most of the events happen based on how you think. Once you shift the mindset, doing the physical part is a lot easier because the mind has decided, *yes, no matter what, I am going to do it.*

We sat him down and impressed upon him how important

it was for him to be a good fielder at the World Cup, and how that would have a positive impact on his career going forward. Credit to him, he was game from ball one, no questions asked.

With strength and conditioning (S&C) coach Shanker Basu and physio Patrick Farhart, we chalked out a good programme, and knew exactly how much to push him. We made a strength programme for that and used fielding for his conditioning. All his running-based work was connected to fielding—all the sprint work over 20, 40, 60 and 80 metres.

Simultaneously, we worked on his catching. We used balls of different colours and weights. We started off with a lighter ball for him to get used to forming that cup and getting the confidence of catching. Slowly, we increased the weight of the ball. We used wet balls and tennis balls. There was a lot of high catching. Finally, we came to the cricket ball. In fact, we got him to do a lot of reverse-cup catching because that is something he was more comfortable with. Surprisingly, for a man of his size, he has got a terrific arm; his ground fielding was fine even then. His throws hit the mitt a lot harder than some of the stronger members of the team.

At the end of it all, Chahal was a catcher transformed. He had a particularly good World Cup, and, subsequently, when we went to New Zealand in 2020, he became one of our main substitute fielders. When somebody comes off the field, generally your twelfth man or whichever reserve batter is the better fielder often goes in. It's not often that you see a leg-spinner running in as a sub. Significantly, the team wanted him out in the middle. It was the captain on the field—Virat led in three games, then Rohit and KL led for one innings—who specifically asked for him, which was, for me, very satisfying. From where he was when he came into the team to being the most wanted fielder in the team on the tour of New Zealand was a tremendous progression. It goes to show that like fitness, fielding is totally controllable. When it comes to batting and bowling, you can work hard, but there are a lot of 'uncontrollables': the nature of the pitch, when you go out to bat, whether edges go to hand, whether catches are taken, whether the Umpire's Call is in your favour. Fielding is not like that. When you work hard, you put in the hard yards, you will see the results on the field; you will see the difference. When the ball comes to you, you are in control. If you work hard, there is no way you will not improve.

One of the biggest challenges for me was to work on all-rounders, like the Jadejas and the Hardiks. Luckily, both are outstanding fielders. But you seldom got time to work with the all-rounders because they were bowling and batting in the nets, and hardly had the energy for fielding. And when I wanted to push them, the science people came in. The S&C and the physios kept saying, 'You need to give him a break. He can't be overworked, give him stationary catches, hit it into his hands, give him a soft ball, don't make him run.' So, when do I work on them? Just for their sake, I ensured that once in two to three net sessions, there was a team fielding session. Otherwise, you couldn't get hold of these guys. It was easy to get hold of the batters and the spinners, but if one was an all-rounder or a fast bowler, it was very difficult because the science team would not allow you to work hard on them.

I am not exaggerating. Mohammed Siraj made his Test debut at the Melbourne Cricket Ground in December 2020, at the end of which one of the S&C guys came to me and said, 'Sri sir, Siraj won't be with you till 7 January. He will be working in the gym. He will not come for any conditioning-related activities. We want him fresh for the Sydney Test.'

I was flabbergasted; after all, Siraj had played just a solitary Test at the time! I told the S&C, 'I am a guy who totally believes in science, but if Siraj drops a catch in Sydney, will you be responsible for it? I am the guy people will be pointing a finger at.' Perhaps

I have a black tongue, because Siraj dropped Steve Smith on cue at the Gabba. He was standing at long-on, not knowing how far he was in from the boundary line. He ran back, was never in control and shelled what by all accounts was a sitter. Luckily, it didn't prove too expensive.

I was fortunate that I had worked with most of the players at the junior level by the time I joined the senior team. There was, therefore, a great degree of comfort with almost everyone right from the off, but like with communication, familiarity is a double-edged sword, too. You must be careful that owing to your closeness, you don't lose sight of the professional side of things. As a coach, you can sometimes get carried away by the trust levels and push the envelope a little too far. That's where having detached attachment, detached familiarity, plays a big part. Even though you know a player very well and feel you can tell him anything, you must still treat him the same as when you met him the first time.

With our own kids, we often make that mistake. Because we are emotionally attached, we tend to push them too far. That's why and when the resentment comes. But if you have a detached attachment, it will help you look from far; it will give you the right perspective. Had Vihari become the captain, for instance, I'd have treated him the same way I did Virat. Just because I know Vihari from when he was seven years old, or that I picked him up from school and took him for practice, didn't mean I could do anything I wanted. I know it's a hypothetical situation, but the point I am trying to make is that you have to give the position of the captain the respect it deserves. Competing at the international level is something most of us can't even comprehend. You must tell the truth; you have to be constructive, but you must know where to draw the line.

As a coach, you may like different players differently and that is human nature. I might like X more than Y, or A more than B because we like some people more than the others, we connect with some more than others. But we must treat everyone equally. Liking someone more should not affect the way you treat them. That is one of the philosophies I try to impress upon other coaches in my seminars.

Having said that, in an environment like the IPL, it is neither easy nor advisable to treat everybody the same. Let's say for instance, you have a Chris Gayle in your team and you have an Arshdeep Singh too, and you can't insist both must have to do a 17.1 in the yo-yo fitness test. You have to give the established players some leeway, depending on what they bring to the table. That's where coaching wisdom and experience comes in—how you handle people of different generations, different cultures. Compromise is possible, maybe even necessary, in franchise cricket, but certainly not on the international stage.

5

THE DYNAMICS OF FIELDING

'You catch with your eyes and you throw with your feet.'

During our three-week vacation in 2021, between the WTC final against New Zealand in Southampton and the start of the Test series against England, I was fortunate to watch top-class fare at Wimbledon alongside my tennis-crazy daughter Ananya.

I chanced upon a few friends as we shuttled from one court to another, and after the usual pleasantries were exchanged, one of them asked me a left-field question. 'How did you manage to retain the fielding coach's position in 2019 even when someone like Jonty Rhodes had thrown his hat into the ring? What was it that gave you the edge?'

To be honest, even though Jonty is a cult figure, I hadn't given it much thought. Instinctively, I said, 'Rishabh Pant.' My friend gaped at me; I could almost hear him think, 'Really? Rishabh Pant?'

It's easier to say this in hindsight, but the focal point of my presentation at the interview had been Rishabh, and I am certain that was the clincher. He was still work in progress at the time, very much so, especially behind the stumps, but I laid out my visions of where he would be over the next two years and how he would get there. Rishabh has that X factor, so to say, in front of the stumps, but I feel one's batting should not paper over the cracks in a wicketkeeper's glovework. We had identified Rishabh as the man to keep wicket across formats by the T20 World Cup scheduled for 2020 and subsequently postponed to 2021, and I outlined the reasons why I felt I could get the next big thing in Indian cricket up to scratch—his skill sets, my rapport with him, as well as my confidence in my coaching ability to get him to a certain level. It was not just about fielding or me having been a good fielder, it was about being able to communicate very well in fielding. I am convinced the way I spoke and the presentation I made on Rishabh tilted the scales in my favour.

I can now reveal that at the time of the interview to the BCCI, which I attended from Antigua, I was reasonably certain that for all practical purposes, MS had played his last match for the country. He hadn't announced it, of course, but I will tell you why I knew. On the morning of the reserve day in our World Cup semifinal against New Zealand in Manchester, I was the first person at the breakfast hall. I was nursing my coffee when MS and Rishabh walked in, picked up their stuff and joined me at my table.

New Zealand had only a couple of overs to bat out and we'd start our innings thereafter, so the match would end reasonably early. Rishabh told MS in Hindi, 'Bhaiyya, some of the guys are planning to leave for London today itself privately. Would you be interested?' MS replied, 'No, Rishabh, I don't want to miss my last bus drive with the team.' I didn't say a word to anyone about this conversation out of sheer respect for the man. He had taken me into confidence. I couldn't shoot my mouth off. So, I didn't utter a word—not to Ravi, not to Arun, not even to my wife.

The point I am trying to make is that by the time of the interview, I knew Rishabh would be MS's natural successor, so to say. By then, Ravi had asked me to get Rishabh up to scratch because he believed the young man would make a difference in both white-ball formats. He wasn't too amused when Rishabh was not picked in the original 15-man squad for the World Cup. That's one of the main reasons why I focussed so much on Rishabh at the presentation. It helped that M.S.K. Prasad, who was the chairman of the selection panel and oversaw the interview, had himself been a wicketkeeper and saw merit in what I had advocated.

Working with wicketkeepers is a major part of the repertoire of a fielding coach when it comes to the Indian team. With so many young keepers coming in with pretty much similar techniques, if you can't coach that aspect, you are a bit of a misfit. We have gone so far down the lane of batters-wicketkeepers that we have stopped thinking of having a keeper-wicketkeeper. Wicketkeeping is seldom seen as part of the fielding coach's job, at least from the outside, but that's far from the case in the Indian team.

Fortunately for me, in my level-two and level-three coaching courses under former England paceman Frank Tyson, my case studies, presentation and thesis, everything was wicketkeeper-oriented. Those conducting the course knew I had been a left-arm spinner; I could bat a bit and I was a good fielder. So, they grilled me on wicketkeeping. Again, luckily, I love coaching wicketkeepers. That, to me, is the most interesting and intriguing part of being a fielding coach. You can do a lot of drills; the sessions can be really good. It's one-on-one most of the time, occasionally two-on-one, which facilitates concentrated personal attention.

When I was at the NCA, Smit Patel, Sanju Samson and Nikhil Naik were my favourites to work with. The likes of Saba Karim, Kiran More and Syed Kirmani, all former Indian stumpers, used to come over as specialist coaches for three days during every camp, and spending time with them was a great learning for me as well. Because of all these things, teaching wicketkeeping became one of my favourite subjects and I enjoyed it as much as I enjoyed working on fielding.

One of the things I had suggested to Rahul Dravid and Saba sometime in 2020 was that we needed to address the issue of wicketkeeping immediately. We can't keep having this argument of 'He is a better batter, no, he is a better keeper'. The wicketkeeping standards of all glovemen across the country should be the same; you can't have different keepers for different conditions. You can't have a situation where Saha is the better keeper than Rishabh for the subcontinent or Sanju is the better fielder than Ishan Kishan, so it's better if Ishan keeps and Sanju fields. No, that should not be the case. The keeping skills should be the same; then, you can pick the better batter, always. Obviously, Rishabh will settle down and the argument of whether to pick the better batter or keeper will be laid to rest, like MS laid it to rest for a decade. What I am saying is we should have a wicketkeeping coach who will work with all the coaches across the country. He will ensure that the wicketkeeping standards in the country are more or less on a par. If A is 9 out of 10, Z should be 8.5 out of 10, so you shouldn't have a problem when it comes to the crunch. Your best 10 or 15 wicketkeepers of the country should be of the same level. That's why you need a wicketkeeping head coach or a wicketkeeping director or whatever you call it. Keeping is an important skill; it can win or lose you matches, we have all seen it happen. We must guard against compromising on wicketkeeping abilities in our desire to play the better batter.

■

Many a time, I have been asked what I look for in a fielder, what first catches my eye. It's a broad question with no one single answer, but the significant traits I seek are athleticism and intent.

Then I focus on hand-eye coordination, ball sense, anticipation and aggression, presence on the field, wanting to create a piece of magic, wanting to make a difference, àla Virat.

When you find a good athlete, it's easier to teach the skills and develop them as opposed to having somebody who is only extremely skillful; it is very difficult to make him into a good athlete. It is a bit of a challenge. It's what the understated but extremely witty John Wright very rightly said to me: 'You can make a donkey into a better donkey, but you can never make a donkey into a horse, no matter how hard you work on it.' If I am looking at a young team, a set of Under-19 boys, I am looking at a good athlete—someone who is quick on the ball, who has got better rotational force and good arm-speed. That's why athleticism and intent rank high on my list of priorities. If you have all the skills but no intent, there is a problem. You are never going to become a good fielder. What kind of intent? Well, intent to create some play on the field; intent to be there and to do something for your team, just the intent to be in that position.

If any kid ticks three of these boxes, teaching him the skills is easy. I feel teaching the technical part is easier; as I have said previously, if you work on your fielding, there is no way you won't get better. Once they have three or four of these qualities, everything else can be taught.

When I say everything else, it largely revolves around technique—the technique of catching, of the slide, the skills which you do on your run, running to your left, running to your right, your underarm, overarm throws, the crow hops, the relay throw and everything else that the coaching manual has. Catching reverse cup, catching normal cup, slip catching, close-in catching, mid-field catching, diving techniques, sliding techniques, all these can always be worked on.

Technique is a very broad term, but if I were to break it down into simple terms, I'd call it the methodology involved in the execution of a certain skill. Skill is the ability to perform a task consistently and repeatedly under pressure. If it is a violin, there is a certain way you have to hold the instrument, a specific way you have to use the strings. That basic philosophy applies to just about anything—music, art, sport. Once you have the core methodology sorted, you can improvise depending on it. That's why I insist that you ignore technique at your own peril. Unless you have the core technique right, it's very difficult to improvise.

I know I said at the beginning that this won't be a technical endeavour, but indulge me a little and let me briefly dwell on a few technical aspects. Such as, in stationary catching, the width of your stance should be slightly more than your shoulder width. If you are standing with a narrow stance, you will struggle to maintain your stability; you will certainly be imbalanced; you will find it challenging to keep your head still. And eventually, you may end up dropping the catch. In throwing, when they say you have to take your feet towards the target in the process of releasing the ball, you have to do it. Otherwise, your throw will not have any power, control or direction, and if one consistently ignores his footwork while throwing, he will soon be on the surgeon's table. If you see those who execute their techniques well, it looks so flawless, so smooth; it looks as if it is the easiest thing in the world, it is pleasing on the eye. Any player with a good technique is very pleasing to the eye—be it batting, bowling or fielding.

Getting the trainees to understand the need to learn, if not master, the basics is part of the coaching process. There are some players who do it naturally, who understand it from a young age. There are others who need to be told. Things like running in straight lines (cutting the angles) and not running in semicircles along the boundary line, understanding the bat angles of different batters in terms of their grip and where the ball is likely to come. Some are good students; they listen and immediately pick it up. Some are naturals; you must leave them alone and not confuse them by giving too many inputs. Again, that varies from player to player. But yes, it is very much coachable and that should be part of the strategy. Having the right fielders in the right position, that is always the objective. Sometimes, it is not possible, but on most occasions, that is the endeavour—to educate and empower the players with the knowledge of what is likely to happen with different angles of bowlers and different set-ups of batters.

When the team is playing so much and a lot of travel and training is involved, it is a challenge occasionally to keep oneself abreast of developments. To better myself and stay in touch with evolving trends, my preferred option is to interact with as many coaches as I can on the circuit. For instance, in the 2018 tour of England, whenever the opportunity presented itself, I sought out James Foster, the former England wicketkeeper. Rishabh was debuting in the third Test and I wanted to talk to Foster to get a hang of things. During the last Test of that series at The Oval, I got him to speak to Rishabh in terms of understanding angles, alignments, and stuff like that. I feel England is a very difficult place to keep wickets. In fact, India and England are the two most challenging places for a wicketkeeper. Period.

Obviously, I keep speaking with Saba Karim; I have a very good relationship with him. The best thing, of course, is to talk to our own Wriddhiman Saha. He is gold, arguably the best wicketkeeper I have ever worked with and a great human being too. If Saha can't, no one can—that's the consensus of the team; that's his reputation as a wicketkeeper. The best masterclass he gave us was in the second Test in Sri Lanka in 2017. On a raging turner at the Sinhalese Sports Club ground, he put on a show one can't forget. We gave him the Team MoM (Man of the Match) for his keeping. Within the team, we would pick who we thought was our Player of the Match, irrespective of who received the official award. Invariably, it's one of the batters or bowlers who walks away with it, but Saha's keeping was so exceptional that to nominate him the Team MoM was a no-brainer. I don't have enough fingers on my hand to count his standout performances behind the stumps, and yet, he is always so unassuming. And since he and Rishabh were both part of the Test squads for an extended period, he was able to watch Rishabh's progression from close quarters. Saha is an astute student of the game and he wouldn't hesitate to tell us whether we were following the right methods to make Rishabh a better keeper and what other tricks we could include to become more efficient. What a team-man!

On the 2018 tour of Australia, we used Parthiv Patel's experience and he was excellent. He'd talk about young keepers, and the techniques and movements involved. In that regard, Parthiv and Dinesh Karthik have been huge assets to the team.

Reading about and listening to podcasts on fielding and keeping helps, too, as also learning from other sports. Having said that, there is a limit to technique. There is a starting point and there is an ending point, and that will not change. But your approach, your knowledge and your awareness, you can keep improving in all these areas. As far as technique is concerned, this is all you do; this is how you do. These are the methods, the skills and the biomechanics involved in wicketkeeping or fielding. If you do all these things correctly, then your technique will more or less take care of itself.

If you take England, the coaching system has undergone a sea change, in my estimation. They don't change an individual too much in terms of technique. It is clear from watching players emerging from the English coaching system that there is too much focus on tactics; that's the focus of most of the coaching in England. For example, take a Dom Sibley or a Rory Burns. They are very good; they understand the tactical aspects of their batting better. But you take them out of their backyard, then good luck. That's because their techniques will not allow them to play spin with any authority. We saw that in India on the 2021 tour. If you don't have the right technique, you have to compensate too much, and you can't always do that unless you are truly special.

There is a lovely phrase in coaching: great sportsmen are great compensators because they know how to compensate for their deficiencies. If Roger Federer feels he is not able to scram to the net to return drop shots, he will keep feeding balls to that area of his opponent's half of the court from where he will not be able to execute the drop shot. Because he doesn't have the energy or the legs to reach and return drop shots, Federer plays a game where he ensures the opponent doesn't drop against him. If he feels he can't last best-of-five sets over seven rounds, his rallies don't go beyond four–five shots; he tries to end the points quickly.

If someone doesn't take his foot out to cover drive, then even if the ball is there for the shot, he will leave it alone, like the great Sachin Tendulkar did in Sydney (2004) during his epic double hundred. He compensated, and brilliantly. As a rule, the more technical faults you have, the more you have to compensate and that becomes a challenge. If you are close to—I am not saying you have to be perfect, no one can be—the technique as you can possibly be, the less you have to compensate for, which means it increases your longevity. Each guy's technique is like his handwriting. No two guys can have the same handwriting, but each can write legibly. It's the same thing with technique. If Laxman plays a cover drive or Rahul Dravid plays a cover drive, they are going to be different. But they are still cover drives, right? And both have their own style. But both are close to the basics.

Obviously, technique is not on top of my list of coaching ingredients, but I will not ignore it. One of the questions that came up during a recent coaching seminar I attended in India was: what is it that stands between a successful Under-19 cricketer and a successful senior India cricketer? Most of the answers were about adapting to conditions, soaking up the pressure, the ability to concentrate more, having the ability to play good balls for longer duration because at the international level, you don't get too many loose balls, while at the Under-19 level, you get the odd loose ball every over, among others. Very few say better technique. Even when they say it, it is only the fifth or sixth observation. But we, as coaches, focus first on technique. We focus on the mechanism, on where the bat is coming from, what's the head position, or how the ball is released and where his arm is. Crucially, in conjunction with the player, you must figure out what is the best technique for that individual.

As a cricketer, you should know your best technique. If Virat keeps his hands on his knees at slip when the ball is delivered, that's because he is very agile; he can go down in a flash. He has the fitness and ability to reach the ball. If Pujara tries the same thing, he won't be as successful. Simple. He has to have his hands below his knees, only then can he catch a ball which is low. Because he has had anterior cruciate ligament issues in both his knees, he will not be able to go down with the same alacrity as Virat, so he has to stay lower from the beginning. You should know your technique, and as a coach, you should know what to coach to whom. That comes with spending time with a player and understanding him.

In the last few years, reverse cup catching has caught on in Indian cricket. Whether you adopt normal cup or reverse cup is situation based. Against the dark night sky or a clear blue sky, when there is no background for you to gauge the depth, the height or the pace at which the ball is coming down, I would ideally prefer the reverse cup. But if there is a cloudy sky and you can assess at some stage, the Indian style or the normal cup is preferred. Both have their advantages and disadvantages.

What I did was allow a player to explore both, give them the options and allow him to judge which is the style best suited to him. But the player should practise both. There could be occasions when you have to do reverse cup. Catching above your head gives you a potential chance; it gives you the opportunity to watch the ball. Even if you are catching with your fingers pointing to the sky, you want to catch it above your eye level. You start the catch above your eyes and finish somewhere near your chest, while you use your elbows as shock absorbers. But that particular point is misinterpreted. People start catching at the chest, which is a big no. Once the ball crosses your eye level, you can never watch it. Getting under the ball early, creating a good base (scissor-feet) and keeping a still head will free up your hands to access the ball better. That's the key to high catching.

We practised reverse cup quite a lot in my last couple of years with the national side. Personally, I think it is the best way to catch, but to each his own and I won't force it on anybody. When Trevor Penney came in, he worked hard on reverse cup. Duncan brought in that South African style a little; I have had conversations with him on this, and I am a believer in reverse cup as well. Even in flat catching, I enjoy a reverse cup because when you want to catch it reverse, your hips have to be low. If the catch is coming at an awkward height, I would rather you take that catch reverse cup because you are low. Once you set yourself up low:

1. You will be able to take some catches which are falling in front of you.
2. You will dive better on either side.
3. It is easier going up than coming down.

I'd give the players live examples by throwing a ball at them at waist height and asking them to catch normal, take a video, then throwing a ball at the same height and asking them to catch reverse cup, so that your knees are almost touching the ground.

As a fielder, you want to be low, especially if you are closer to the bat. The closer you are to the bat, the lower you should be.

▪

I had an excellent conversation with Rahul Dravid during the lockdown in 2020. It revolved around youngsters coming into the team. I was quite perplexed that young batters had no idea of doing a silly point or a short leg. Suddenly, they come into the Indian team, and when they have to stand at short leg to an Ashwin or silly point to Jadeja and Axar, they have no clue where they should stand if the ball is turning or is not turning. That, if Ashwin is bowling stump line to a right-hander, the ball is likely to come to your right at forward short leg. If he is bowling outside the off stump, the catch might come straight to you or to your left.

What came out of that conversation was that most of our kids—let's say someone like a Prithvi Shaw or a Shubman Gill—haven't had any prior experience of standing in these positions. Right from the age of nine or thereabouts, Prithvi has been the star of his team, whichever team he has played in. Right from that time, he has fielded in the position he wanted to because whoever was the coach of that team was happy to allow Prithvi to do his bidding. If Prithvi said he wanted to field in the covers, the coach would be okay with it. If he wanted to do gully, the coach wouldn't object. He grew up like that, fielding at a position of his choice. And suddenly, he comes to the Indian team and lo and behold: you have to stand at short leg for Ashwin.

That is the superstar culture with which some of the young batters are coming in. The same goes for Shubman. He would have done the same thing with Punjab—comfort fielding, mid-on, mid-off. When they come into the Indian team, they are not equipped to stand close-in in front of the bat. Contrary to popular perception, not everyone is a finished product as a fielder when they come into the Indian team, and all the more so now. I saw this trend in my last two or three years with the Indian team. I don't know if that superstar culture is a good thing or a bad thing, but it is happening. When K.L. Rahul broke through in 2014, I used to push him to do silly point and short leg when he was not wicketkeeping because I already knew him well, and he did it. But the mindset is different in the guys coming in now. Some are just not very willing to put in the hard work.

In Ahmedabad during the last Test against England in March 2021, things came to a boil with Shubman. I contemplated having a word with Ravi about it, but held my horses and took him out for lunch instead. I told him, 'You are considered the next big thing. People are looking at you from a leadership perspective. As a future leader, the one thing you should bring is inspiration. You should have a presence on the field and when you do something, you must do it with intent. It is not just doing it for the sake of the team. Do it for yourself. Do it for your satisfaction, not because the captain wants you there. What you do there should be an inspiration for the whole team.'

Then, I illustrated the point with examples. 'Keaton Jennings came to India in 2016 with the England team. He played in only the last two Tests, but every ball of those two games—we made 631 and 759 in our only innings in those two matches—he stood at short leg,' I pointed out. 'Ollie Pope stood at short leg for the entire 2021 series. I have a problem here when, after one session, you say your calf is paining, your hamstring is hurting. How come they are able to do it and you are not? They stood at short leg a lot longer than you did. To me, that is a problem.' It's the same thing with Prithvi and Vihari. Vihari comes out of lockdown, stands at short leg for three Test matches in Australia and pulls his hamstring. I know that injury was multifactorial, but it was also indicative of poor fitness. Since 2016, I'd call up

Mayank Agarwal and Vihari, wherever they were playing, and ask them to not ignore sessions of short leg fielding. But with some of the guys who popped up from the Under-19 level towards the end of my stint with the Indian team, I didn't know what to do. This culture has to change.

In a way, that is one of the pitfalls of fast-tracking Under-19 boys to long-format international cricket. If Laxman didn't do short leg or silly point while playing Ranji Trophy for Hyderabad in his formative years, or Rahul for Karnataka, Kanwaljit Singh (the veteran off-spinner) and Anil wouldn't have spared them. No one does this to these younger guys. Some of them get into the Test team with a string of good performances in white-ball cricket. Standing in slips in Australia or England and in short leg in India is the most difficult challenge, and they are singularly unprepared for it. I do have a serious problem with the way things are developing. The solution is: it must go from top to bottom, that's the only way things work in India. It has to go through the NCA. Otherwise, it will snowball into a serious problem. If we really want to stay on top in Test cricket, the culture has to change. You can't keep shifting short leg fielders every two hours; it is not a lottery, it is a specialist position.

People think the newest or the youngest member of a team is plonked at silly point or short leg as a matter of convenience. But it's not a 'Put a lid on him, make him stand at the most exposed positions' scenario. There is a reason why the youngest guy is given that slot. He is expected to have better reflexes than someone who is 33 or 34. He is expected to be fitter, and, therefore, able to stand there for a longer period of time without losing concentration. These are things you expect when a youngster comes in—that he will bring in energy and a certain level of fitness, which will inspire others. I believe it is the youngsters who inspire the seniors rather than the other way round.

At these two positions, you need extraordinary hand-eye

coordination and the concentration of a batter. The lower the centre of gravity, the better they move, which is why the shorter guys usually don these roles. Someone like Prithvi has amazing skills to be a good short leg fielder. It's just that he has to develop the intent.

A taller fielder has a larger wingspan, which will help if you are at third slip or gully. But at short leg, it is all about moving quickly and anticipating. You only become a good close-in fielder if you have fielded in that particular position consistently over a period of time. If you notice, in the beginning, it was a challenge for us to get a settled slip cordon because there were too many changes in the team. Sometimes M. Vijay was playing, sometimes Shikhar Dhawan was playing, sometimes Pujara was playing. You had so many different guys coming in and going out, it was difficult to nail down the slip fielders. But in my last couple of years, as the batting unit took more concrete shape, we had a good slip cordon, with regulars manning specific positions. Our conversion percentage was 83, much better than what it used to be, but yes, we could have got it up to 90.

Specialized fielding positions require specific drills, too. Even your fitness regimen needs to be customized. If you are a fast bowler, it's recommended that you do a half squat and go 90 degrees. But if you are a wicketkeeper or you are going to do a lot of silly point or short leg, I would say your squat should be ass to grass. It must be a full squat because that is the position you are going to be standing in for most part of the day. There will be a subtle difference in your training programme and practice regimen.

However, the most important thing is fielding in that position consistently. Yes, there is a fear of getting hit. There is too much at stake for the youngsters coming in now. They don't want to miss an IPL because they have got hit at short leg or broken a leg, but that can happen even in the outfield. I get the feeling kids don't like to field close-in nowadays as opposed to the earlier days, when there was the fear of seniors, if nothing else. It used to be more of an old-fashioned operational style. I truly believe cricketers learn from the senior players in the team more than they do from the coaches. When we played, we had a very strong set of senior players. It's not as if that isn't the case any more, but there is not enough exchange of information when it comes to fielding. It happens only when there is a need, only when there is a necessity. Otherwise, everybody is in his own space.

I have alluded previously to Chahal's excellent arm. Where does the strength in a throw come from? Quite simply, the entire body. There is a beautiful quote in fielding. 'You catch with your eyes and you throw with your feet.' Throwing is all about footwork, as is catching. There is so much footwork involved in fielding. Once your feet are in the right place, it allows your body and hands to move freely and generate force. Throwing is all about your feet. And catching is all about the eyes. How the eyes have to be steady; how they are the camera of the body. I sometimes tell the boys, 'If I take a picture on the mobile and my hand is shaking, will you like it? Of course not, because the picture will be blurred. Similarly, when you are in the field, your body must be still as the ball hits the bat. Only then will you be able to get a clear picture and anticipate better. Your eyes have to be still when the ball is in the air, only then will you be able to catch it.' The eyes can move in one plane, but they should not be bobbing up and down. For that, the positioning of the feet is very important.

During one early practice session on our last tour of England, I noticed that Avesh Khan was all over the place so far as alignment was concerned while throwing the ball. I told him that in the absence of alignment and sync while throwing, it wouldn't be long before he picked up a serious injury. 'If you want to have a long career, pay a little attention to your technique,' I said. I knew that if I told him to cock his wrist and get his elbow over his shoulder, he won't understand what I was trying to convey— likewise with a Mohammed Siraj. I couldn't tell him to get his wrist to snap to improve his throwing technique, because he wouldn't have got it. Instead, I urged him to throw the ball to me on the bounce from wherever he was. To do so, you must get your arm above your shoulder; you have to get it close to your head. He started throwing one-bounce and the arm automatically got better. That's all I wanted.

At the end of the day, as coaches, we look for results. With some people, you can't throw jargon around. I can go to a Pujara or an Ashwin and say you need to use your wrist a little more. They understand it. But that doesn't work with some others. At the end of the day, you must speak their language for optimal results.

6

THE MAN-MANAGERS

*'Bloody hell, will you satiate your hunger here itself or
will you save some of it for wickets, too?'*

At the elite level, 'coaching' is a bit of a misnomer.
As a coach, you will suggest subtle changes, minor
refinements to problems that creep in subconsciously.
You won't talk at length about high left elbows and playing close
to the body, getting the head on top of the ball or having a
still head. You won't harp on the position of the left foot or the
angle of seam at the time of delivery. These are all elements you
address at the junior levels; by the time these athletes graduate
to playing for the country, in most cases, the basics are well
ingrained in them.

More than coaching, I'd say, at the elite performance platform, a
coach graduates into a man-manager. Yes, he will strategize because
modern-day sport thrives on back-room work. Yes, he will offer
technical inputs when required because, as I said, mistakes can
grow on you when you are constantly on the move and playing
matches, and, therefore, don't have enough time or energy to
go back to the drawing board for self-introspection. But at the
end of the day, it's how you optimize your resources and what

environment you offer them that will allow them to flourish, and that's most crucial.

What really is man-management? It's about keeping each person in the best space available within that environment where performance is not forced out of that individual but becomes inevitable. It's about keeping them in the right mental space and coaching them in a way that they feel they are becoming a better version of themselves.

Man-management is about helping a player be the best they can be at a particular point of time. At the same time, they are learning, becoming a better player without feeling the stress of having to take too much on board. It's about giving them the right options, empowering them technically, mentally, emotionally and physically—essentially in all aspects of the sport.

There's no secret to being a good man-manager. You have to understand the other person, what they are looking for. You need to know the ideal situation they want to be in. It's about being aware of their energies and using their own energies to get the best out of them. You don't necessarily have to be born a good man-manager. You can become better at it by learning from your mistakes, as most of us do.

As coaches and leaders, we take so many decisions; out of these, a fair few are wrong. We should not overlook the fact that cricket is a sport of failures. In fact, not only cricket, all sport is about how you fail more than you succeed. But if you can mine those failures—mine as in digging out—and learn from them, then you become more efficient in man-management, in tactical planning, your decision-making and your responsibility as a leader. All these things improve slightly.

Coming back to the basic question of whether it is inborn or acquired, man-management is part inherent and part a learned or acquired skill. If someone is willing to learn from the errors he's made, then it is definitely a learned skill. If they're willing to read or willing to look at other coaches who've done it well and pick up nuances, then it's a learned skill. Let me put it this way—if you're coaching the sport, then it becomes more challenging to be a man-manager. But if you're coaching the person, then it becomes a little easier to be a good man-manager because then you understand the person. Once you understand the person, you can get a little more help in making the right decision for that person.

Sport is just a medium to coach the person. You coach the person; cricket is the medium here in our case. If you're looking at coaching in that fashion, if that is your coaching philosophy, then you'll end up being a better man-manager than if you're coaching only the sport. If you're just going there coaching the sport, you'll sometimes overlook the person you're coaching; everything can become very matter of fact and that may not make you a very good man-manager.

Let's get into specifics to see if I can make more sense. So here we are in Sydney at the beginning of 2019, having just won a fantastic Test in Melbourne to grab the series lead going into the final game. We had played three very high-intensity Tests, which were not just physically and technically demanding but also very strenuous on the mind. There was forecast for rain for the last two days of the Test in Sydney, so we just needed to make sure we didn't do anything silly over the first two-and-a-half days, so that we could create history and come back from Australia with our first series victory there in 71 years.

Fortunately, Virat won the toss and our batters got to work. Pujara did what he had done all tour, the others all weighed in and Rishabh smashed an outstanding 100 against the dispirited Aussies to muscle us past 600. It was pretty much game over, series in the bag, rain or no rain.

By the end of day two, Australia's openers had reached 24 without loss. In the evening, Bumrah sought out Arun for a chat.

'Sir,' he started, slightly hesitantly, 'the wicket is absolutely placid, and there is nothing in it for the faster bowlers.'

One of Arun's many strengths is his willingness to listen. He knew Bumrah wanted to tell him something but wasn't unsure how to go about it. But instead of forcing his hand, Arun allowed things to play out naturally. Bumrah, of course, had been the star of India's win in the previous Test; he had been our best bowler throughout the series, as a matter of fact.

'I am very jaded, Sir, physically exhausted and mentally drained,' he went on. 'That's where I am at, personally. There's nothing at stake so far as the series is concerned. The track is docile. It's more or less certain that this game will end in a draw.'

After this elaborate build-up, the coin finally dropped. 'So what I will do, Sir, is I'll bowl a little slowly. I won't go flat out. I'll bowl well within myself and take out this Test.'

One of the items that was top on our priority list was workload management. We were going from Australia to New Zealand for a white-ball series and Bumrah had already been rested for that. We wanted him to go back to India, take a break, refresh himself and be ready for the World Cup, which was just five months away.

Arun heard him out with total commitment. What I mean is that he wasn't thinking when Bumrah was speaking. The problem with thinking as someone is speaking is that you are already formulating your response and therefore likely to miss the tone or the import of the speaker. After listening to Bumrah's opinion with full attention and intent, Arun spoke firmly but gently, outlining two options that lay ahead of Bumrah.

'The first option is what you are saying,' Arun pointed out. 'You can take it easy and bowl well within yourself. You can bowl at 130–32 kmph, just finish playing this Test, then fly back home to recover and get ready for the World Cup. But in doing so, what may happen is you may end up giving the batter the confidence that he has played you well. You have bowled slowly; you have bowled within yourself; you have controlled your pace because you didn't want to exert your body and mind. But the batter doesn't know that. So, if you bowl like that and if a player like Shaun Marsh or Marnus Labuschagne plays you out, he will actually get the confidence to do it again. He's going to go one-up over you. So, tomorrow, in another match, even when you are bowling flat out, he will think, "I have played him well, I have that mental edge over him." That will give him the confidence to play you better even if you're bowling at your best. He will get accustomed to you.

'The second option is to go out there and bowl another spell or two of four or five overs each, wherein you go flat out and give nothing away to the batter even on a placid track. By doing that, you will also give the impression that even on a totally docile strip on day three or day four of the fourth Test of a series that you have all but won, you're still able to come and do this. Assume that sometime later, you are bowling to the same batter in another game on day one when there's a little bit of assistance. You look at the psychological edge you will have over that batter when the conditions are more favourable to you. You can either do what you are saying or choose the second option I have outlined. The choice is yours.'

Arun knew Bumrah to be a very sensitive person. He's always handled Bumrah with care—what you tell him and how you say it. He doesn't like to be hit. If you see his body language when he's hit, when he comes back and takes a wicket, you know that his pride has been wounded. Even when he drops a catch or misfields, he's very upset with himself. He's very cross; till he gets it back, he's not the kind of guy who's going to sleep well.

The longer Arun spoke, the more I noticed that Bumrah's face had gone from being in intent conversation to an almost lost look. He was gazing into the oblivion and I had seen him enough to understand that he was in deep thought. To me, it seemed as if Bumrah was thinking to himself, '*Yeh meri dimaag mein kyun nahi aaya?* (Why didn't I think of this?)'

Then he said, 'Yes, Sir, I agree with you. Thank you very much for telling me this. I'll go and give my best. I anyway have a one-month break after this. I will do what I have to do. I am not going to hold back when it comes to that.'

Bumrah isn't just sensitive, he is also a very proud performer. He had bowled spiritedly on day three without any success; day four started belatedly. It had rained in the morning and there was no play until lunch. When we finally got out, it was extremely humid and hot, almost like Chennai or Mumbai. He went out there, took the second new ball and bowled a brilliant spell. It was sheer bad luck that he only got Peter Handscomb's wicket during that burst. I know Kuldeep Yadav bowled beautifully and got five wickets, but Bumrah was something else that afternoon.

When he came back into the dressing room at tea time, he went straight to Arun and told him, 'You were right, Sir. From now on, I will go all out, no matter the game situation.' Like we say, *Sher bhukha mar jayega lekin ghaas nahi khayega* (A lion might die of hunger but will never eat grass). Bumrah is a bit like that; he has great pride in what he does.

A fast bowler, any bowler, needs to have that kind of pride. 'I understand where you're coming from, Sir,' he continued. 'You have triggered a change in my thought process. I will take this as a learning and stick to this going forward.'

I thought this was just terrific from Arun—a master lesson in man-management. Without attempting to instruct him, without Bumrah even realizing, Arun got the best out of him by outlining various options and patiently pointing out the potential ramifications of each of them. The job of a coach is to empower the player and also to give him the right feedback and choices.

Ultimately, at elite-level coaching, it is for the player to decide which part he wants and what decisions he wants to make.

A part of man-management is giving the player the right options, showing him what you think is the right way. If you provide the options in the appropriate method, in the right tone, by showing him the right picture, then at least nine times out of 10, if not 10 times out of 10, the player will choose the right option. That is when you win as a coach. That is man-management.

■

The word 'coach' is an interesting one. What is coaching? Where did 'coach' come from? The way I look at it, it came from 'carriage'. Whether it is a railway coach or the carriage of a horse, it takes you from one place to another. The sports coach takes you from one place to another, be it in your career or your life. That journey could be from the age of eight to 35, or it could be a period of three years, or it could just be six months.

The job of a coach is to take the player from one place to a better place. The other job of a coach is to make a player think he is better than he is. There is a nice quote in our coaching forum: 'A good coach is one who makes the player think great about him. A great coach is one who makes a player think great about himself.'

Most of the time as coaches, we make the mistake of wanting to go there and impress the player and make them think, 'Arre yeh achcha coach hai (He is a good coach).' In the ideal concept of coaching, of which man-management is a massive part, one must make a player think highly about himself.

That day, Bumrah went back thinking highly of himself. He knew that on a flat track on a hot day after three-and-a-half Test matches, he could hurry the likes of Marsh, Labuschagne and Travis Head, or whoever for that matter.

A coach has to wear many hats; you have to keep changing them like a circus clown. You have to juggle hats. But obviously, one of the key roles of a coach at this level is man-management.

Arun or I don't have to teach Bumrah how to bowl a yorker. Arun has set it up in such a way in the last few years that Bumrah can deliver a yorker whenever he wants to. So, you don't teach them to play cricket any more; instead, you teach them subtle things. Obviously, when you go a few levels down (at the junior levels), it is different.

Each guy is different. We just spoke about Bumrah—extreme pride, extreme sensitivity. Mohammed Shami is totally at the other end of the spectrum. Don't get me wrong; it is not that he is not proud or he is insensitive. It's just that he is bindaas, with the devil-may-care attitude.

We were in South Africa in early 2018, for the first Test in Cape Town. Within half an hour of the start of the game, Bhuvi reduced them to 12 for three, dismissing Dean Elgar, Aiden Markram and Hashim Amla. Then we bowled like millionaires, and they ended up making 286. That evening, Ravi summoned the pace attack (Bhuvi, Shami, Bumrah and Hardik) and thundered, 'What's this rubbish? I have seen so much driving in the middle that I am sick of it. From this point on, whatever driving happens must be only on the road. No bloody half-volleys, get stuck into them.'

We lost Cape Town. We couldn't chase down 208 which was ridiculous. Then we lost Centurion, another match we should have won and where we could have been 2-0 up or at worst 1-1. We had already surrendered the series when we went to Johannesburg for the final Test.

We did the unthinkable by choosing to bat because we felt the conditions would only get worse for batting as the game wore on. Shami didn't turn up for the first innings—he went one for 46 from 12 overs, and then on the fourth day, he was again reasonably inconspicuous till tea, by which time South Africa appeared on course for victory. Needing 241, they had reached 136 for three when the lads trooped in for tea break.

Shami looked disinterested as he came back in, like he did at lunch, when he had piled up his plate with rice and mutton curry. During the first interval, Ravi had lost his shirt after one glance at Shami's plate. 'Bloody hell, will you satiate your hunger here itself or will you save some of it for wickets, too?' he shouted.

In his typically laconic, laid-back fashion, Shami drawled, '*Haan, haan, yahan bhi kha lunga, udhar bhi kha lunga* (Yes, yes, I will eat here and I will eat there, too).'

We all shared Ravi's frustrations because this was a series that ought to have played out differently. It looked as though for all our toils, we would have nothing to show. Just before Shami left the dressing room to return for the post-tea session, Ravi took him aside and wound him up. Not by telling him he was a match-winner and stuff like that, but by reminding him of the lunch-time conversation and Shami's promise.

Post-tea, he was unplayable. He blasted through the middle and lower order to finish with five for 28, and we ended up winning by a comfortable 63-run margin. As he sauntered back into the changing room, he grinned wickedly, '*Haan, merko aur gussa dilao aap log. Merko gaali do. Utna gussa nahi dilate jitna dilaana chahiye* (Yes, please make me more angry. You people should curse me. You don't make me as angry as you should).'

If Shami took the 'curses' in his stride, it was because of the rapport he enjoyed with Ravi. When he was going through domestic turmoil, with his wife slapping a case and everything being played out in the media, the first person Shami called was Ravi, during the Nidahas Trophy in Sri Lanka in 2018. He told Ravi, '*Yeh maine kuch nahi kiya* (I didn't do any of these things).' He wanted to have Ravi's faith because he knew this could affect his career.

Ravi immediately called up his people in Mumbai, who in turn fixed things up for Shami in Kolkata for him to take things forward. Ravi invested a lot of time in Shami, constantly speaking to him and reassuring him that it would not affect his career. His advice to him was to buy time, completely stay low, desist from making any remarks in public or even private, and follow all legal protocols as advised by his lawyer.

A few months down the line, in June 2018, before the Test against Afghanistan in Bengaluru, there was a fitness test, which Shami understandably failed big time. Dispirited and dejected, he told Ravi at our hotel in Bengaluru, '*Mein cricket chod dunga. Meri career khatam ho gayi* (I will quit cricket. My career is finished).'

Not only had he failed the fitness test, his Dexa score was also not very good. The Dexa test ascertains one's body fat, for which we do a scan that reveals the area of the body the fat is concentrated in. In other words, what you have to work on in terms of fitness. It gives you details about fat percentage and muscle percentage, so that you know whether you are actually muscular or if you're looking strong because of your fat. You get a lot of insights; unfortunately, none of his test results were great.

Ravi shot back, '*Achcha. Phir tu cricket chod dena chahtha hai toh chod de. Lekin tu karega kya chodke?* (Okay. If you want to quit cricket, then quit. But what will you do after quitting?),' with a few expletives thrown in. 'Can you give commentary? Of course not. Can you get into coaching? No, you can't. *Padai karegaa?* (Will you study?). And because of what's going on about you in the media, no political party will be willing to touch you.' He said all this in Hindi, in a manner Shami could understand and relate to. After the last comment on politics, Shami burst out laughing.

Then, Ravi outlined the options he had in mind for Shami. He went on, 'Look, forget about this Afghanistan Test. In any case, given your condition, you won't survive even one day. I need you for the England tour [a couple of months later]. For

With Hanuma Vihari after his century at Sabina Park, Kingston. Ours is an association that started way back in 2003

Suits always make for attractive men...

With Sir Vivian Richards—a pure fanboy moment! Well, the night ended in the wee hours

Pranking around the streets of Wellington, New Zealand, with R. Ashwin

In high spirits at the Melbourne Cricket Ground changing room after our dramatic win in 2020–21

With the coveted Border–Gavaskar Trophy, which we won in back-to-back series in Australia, making us the first Asian team to do so

Celebrating Test wicket No. 400 with the champion!

Lord's mein jab Test jeete hain, selfie toh banta hai! *(A win at Lord's calls for a selfie!). At the historic balcony in 2021 with my partners in crime*

With 'Captain Cool' M.S. Dhoni

With the legend Dhoni after he announced his Test retirement. Both our eyes are bright with to-be-shed tears

About to receive a shawl from His Holiness the Dalai Lama. My grateful thanks to the Himachal Pradesh Cricket Association and Anurag Thakur for this priceless opportunity

Another group photo post a bilateral series win

At work

At the Lord's balcony during my first international match there

In Cape Town in 2018, after India's first-ever ODI series win on South African soil. It wasn't just a win, we beat them 5-1

Proud and satisfied coaches in the Gabba change rooms with the Border–Gavaskar Trophy

With Bharat Arun, my friend, mentor and teacher

A customary travel selfie with K.L. Rahul

DK's heroics in the final of the Nidahas Trophy are the stuff of legend. Here's one with him for the album post the adrenaline rush

Who do you think is talking?

With the man who makes fielding coaches look better than they are. Arguably the best in the world in his era, Ravindra Jadeja

The great thing about Ashwin is that he is an exceptionally good student of the game

I knew MS had played his last match for India. Didn't want to miss this moment. Seen here after the heartbreaking loss to New Zealand in the 2019 World Cup semifinals

With K. Srikanth, former World No. 1 men's singles badminton player, at a sports journalists' awards function in Hyderabad

One of the many quiet dinners with Virat and the gang on our away tours. It's very rare to get a quiet evening with this superstar

All the coaches seen here with Suman, on the extreme right with his son. Suman always extended us the best hospitality while we were in Adelaide, pampering us with unconditional love and support. This picture is after the Adelaide Test win in the 2018–19 series

Some relaxed moments…

One of the most complete fielders I have seen and worked with, Suresh Raina

Behind the team's fearless brand of cricket was Ravi doing the tough talking

Rishabh Pant and I had developed a great working relationship. Almost twinning here ahead of the WTC finals in Southampton

Here, the background is more important than the people

A trip to Thiruvananthapuram (or Trivandrum) is never complete without offering our prayers to Lord Vishnu in the 2,000-year-old Anantha Padmanabhaswamy Temple

An evening at Oulton Park, Leeds, with my wife, Vijayalakshmi

Subjected to a selfie by Ananya, my adorable daughter

that, I am ready to throw my weight behind you. What do you think? You think you'll be ready for England?'

There were four of us in Ravi's suite during this conversation. Ravi turned to Patrick Farhart, our physio, and asked him, 'Patrick, what do you think? Do you think you can get him ready for England?' Patrick was confident that if Shami plunged himself into training, he would easily make the cut for the tour of England.

Emboldened by the physio's words, Ravi continued in Hindi, 'We will do anything for Shami. You don't worry about anything. Be with the NCA for the next two months. We will have a physio and a trainer dedicated to you. Work hard for the next few weeks; come to England for my sake. The first Test starts on 4 August; we are now in May. You have the whole of June and July at your disposal. We will look after you for two months, but you must cooperate with us, too. Get ready and take out all your rage and frustrations on the England batters. Whoever you have angst against, channel all that against England.'

Now, that's the language Shami understands. If Ravi had spoken to Shami like Arun had with Bumrah, I don't think it would have had the desired effect. If you use even one abusive word, the sensitive Bumrah would rush out of the room. That's what man-management is all about. You have to choose your words and your intonation very wisely. You can't talk to Bumrah like you can to Shami.

Ravi didn't just stop at that. Having promised him all the support, he went one step further by speaking to the BCCI and restoring Shami to the central contracts pool. His IPL contract was also not impacted, his lawyers saw to that. I don't think Shami had any doubts that Ravi would stick by his word, but to see the head coach move heaven and earth to ensure his best interests were taken care of at a difficult time must have made a massive impact on him.

That was the motivation for Shami. So, he came to the NCA

and worked his backside off for six to eight weeks. After this episode, his relationship with Ravi, and by extension Arun, was transformed. Shami knew there was a line he must not cross, but from that point, they became friends as much as coaches and wards. They could say anything to each other without fear of being misunderstood, but Ravi and Arun ensured their personal relationship didn't affect the professional demands and Shami was smart enough to figure out that there was no way he could get away by cutting corners.

From then on, Shami practically ate out of Ravi's and Arun's hands. When he made a mistake, he would be the first to put his hand up and admit to the same. He knew when to push himself, when the team needed him to set fatigue aside and stretch the boundaries of his limits. If you wanted him to go flat out in the final hour of the fourth evening of the third Test of a long series, he would smile and say, '*Chalo, Sir, yeh kar dunga mein* (Sure, Sir, I will do this).' He was absolutely magical on the tour of England, and at the World Cup, too.

This is the man who was so affected by the events around him that he wanted to quit the game. Had it not been for mentors or man-managers in the form of Ravi and Arun at that stage, I am not sure the cricket world would have been able to enjoy his extraordinary skills in the last few years.

For someone like me, watching from close quarters, it was a great lesson in man-management. Ravi had to go beyond the sport to make Shami feel at home at the most difficult time of his life. It becomes incumbent on you to make people comfortable even outside of the team environment if you want them to deliver their best. Once they know that you have their back, that you are willing to walk the extra mile for their sake, more than half the battle is won.

Options—now that's a beautiful word, a must-have in the lexicon of every coach or man-manager. It's about giving the players choices and helping them select the best of those. There was a time when Rishabh Pant was getting out in a certain way, charging and being caught at deep cover or deep point. That was early on in his career, around 2018, but he subsequently managed to minimize being dismissed in that fashion.

However, another issue crept in. Rishabh is an instinctive, compulsive stroke-maker. In the first Chennai Test against England in February 2021, he went after Jack Leach's left-arm spin, smashing him for several towering sixes. But in his desire to dominate, he often let his heart take over, with predictably disastrous results.

He sought Ravi out during the middle of the series and said, 'Sir, I am getting out stumped, caught in the deep... What are my options?'

Rishabh isn't someone who likes to be moved away from his style of play. If you tell him, 'Don't hit in the air, playing along the ground, look for singles and twos,' not only will he not like it, he will cease to be Rishabh Pant. He's not someone who likes to be curbed of his natural ability.

Ravi knew this, of course. In a language that would resonate with Rishabh, with more than the odd cuss word thrown in, he said, 'They have four fielders on the leg-side boundary. You might be able to clear them nine times out of 10, but even if you hit one in the air in that direction and are caught, what's the point in that? *Tu ek kaam kar na, tu wohi ball ko reverse sweep maar. Tere liye point he nahi hain* (Do one thing, reverse sweep the same ball, there is no point fielder for you). When the left-arm spinner is bowling without a point, reverse sweep him. A decent connection will get you four and if you hit it really well, it will go for a six.'

Rishabh was grinning like a Cheshire cat. '*Sir, aise options de diya karo, badhiya hai* (Sir, do give these kinds of options. They are very good). I didn't even think about this. Now I will reverse sweep him; even if he pitches it in the rough, I will reverse him.' Of course, Rishabh being Rishabh, he took that suggestion too much to heart and started to reverse the faster bowlers also, men like James Anderson and Jofra Archer!

Even someone as accomplished as Ravi had made mistakes in the past but was quick to learn from them and readjust his focus. Sometimes, you try to change the basic character of an individual and almost without fail, that doesn't work. Ravi realized that the only way to get Rishabh to perform at his best was to allow him to play in his natural, aggressive way but give him more run-scoring options because that's what appeals to him. Understanding a player's psyche, understanding them as a person, becomes more significant than understanding the sportsman in a person and that makes one a good man-manager.

At the same time, it is important to not lose sight of the fact that you are there to do a job, not win a popularity contest. We have all fallen into the trap of wanting players to like us; at least I can speak for myself—that I should be popular among the players. If you want to be liked, sometimes you may not end up taking the right decisions for the team. That's another lesson I learned from Ravi.

I made the mistake of trying to get everyone to like me, giving them what they wanted, but Ravi doesn't care whether they like him or not. With Ravi, only one thing matters—the Indian cricket team. Zero agenda. If he identified someone who he thought brought the X factor and added value to the team, he would back him to the hilt. But at the end of the day, if that individual was not performing, he would let go of him after a decent run because the team was more important to him than any individual. He was very clear on that. He didn't say it all the time, but it was evident from the way he went about performing his role as a head coach of the Indian cricket team. When you have a mindset like that, when you're loyal to the Indian cricket team, then all the questions about whether or why you are liked or not liked by a player don't arise at all. He could care a damn for that.

That is the lesson I picked up—where are your loyalties as a coach? What is your role? As long as you understand that and you make your decision, you help players align to that thought process; the bigger picture will take care of itself.

7

OF CAPTAINS AND LEADERS

'If everyone fears the Indian team now, it's because of our approach as much as our skills. Take it or leave it, that's your call.'

In no other team sport does a captain have a more influential decision-making role than in cricket. I don't mean any disrespect to those who sport the captain's armband in, say, a hockey or football team. But where a football or hockey captain can only inspire with his deeds, a cricket captain is more than someone who merely walks out for the spin of the coin.

Just sticking with football and hockey, the planning and strategizing is done off the field, by the manager or the coach who formulates ideas with respect to formations, man-marking, approaches, substitutions, and the like. The captain is just another player for the most part. Things couldn't be any different in cricket.

It's not as if the back-room staff don't have much of a contribution to make. If anything, in the T20 format, the cricket coach plays pretty much the same role as the football manager, though even in that variant of the sport, the captain has to make instantaneous decisions. The longer the format, the more intricate is the role of the captain—be it when it comes to field placements, bowling changes or deciding which bowler comes on from which end.

Simply put, the captain is the central figure on the park when the team is fielding. He is the one directing traffic and therefore it is imperative that every player has one eye on him all the time.

It goes without saying that every captain is a leader, too. Leadership traits manifest themselves differently in different individuals. Some like the attention; they thrive and feed off it, like Virat. They are full of energy and intensity; they don't mind being in your face; they use the captain's tag to excellent effect. And then there are those like MS—actually, strike that. There is, after all, no one quite like MS.

So much has been said about MS that I don't want to fall into the trap of being boringly repetitive. His calmness under pressure, the ability to mask his emotions and the speed with which he arrives at calculated game plans are obvious characteristics that have been widely eulogized. But having worked at close quarters with MS for nearly five years, the one thing that has fascinated me is the loyalty he has been able to command from all comers.

That was one of his main strengths as a leader, even though he never went out of his way to attract loyalty. MS treated people—players as well as support staff—in such a way that you organically developed loyalty not only towards him but also towards whatever he did.

MS is a great teacher without attempting to be one. One of the many pithy messages he sent out, and which made a deep impact on me, was to never want anything too much. His philosophy was simple: when you want something too much or too badly, you get attached to it. Once that happens, emotion comes between you and what you are trying to achieve. His view was that if you want something too much, you should find a way of letting go of it and strike a middle path where you develop detached attachment. That was something he often stressed during team meetings.

Even during his last pre-match meeting as a Test captain, one of the things MS told the team was, 'When it comes to Test cricket, the problem with some of you is that you want it too badly. If you want something that bad, you tend to overthink and over-analyse; you tend to get a little stiff and your body is not at its best. You have to let go, then you can see the results for yourself.'

None of us knew at the time that MS would retire after the Melbourne Cricket Ground Test in 2014, but that was him. He could have gone on and played at least a hundred Tests if he wanted to, but he was never fascinated by or attached to numbers and statistics. That's why when he spoke about not getting obsessed with things to the exclusion of everything else, it immediately registered because he didn't preach anything that he didn't practise.

Commanding loyalty isn't an easy accomplishment, it's just a really tough process. But for MS, it came effortlessly. One of the main reasons for that was the way he conducted himself, not just within the cricketing environment but outside of it as well. He is just such a good person, that it's impossible not to like him from the off.

MS is a great exponent of focussing on the small things, on doing them right. Primary among them was not criticizing anyone openly or harshly. It's not that he didn't read the riot act, but he didn't make a song and dance of it. He is of the view that the intention is to get the player to be a better version of himself, not to make them feel small, slighted or belittled by being hauled over the coals in public. I am not saying that's the only way to go about things, but that was the preferred mode of operation so far as MS was concerned, which obviously worked exceptionally well for him.

Like good coaches—beyond a point, MS was no longer just a leader, a captain or a player, he had transcended all this—he also gave people options to better themselves without losing sight of the bigger picture. One of the pitfalls of being immersed in the unforgiving cauldron of international sport is that sometimes, you forget the reason why you embraced the sport in the first place—that is to have fun. MS kept reminding young and old alike that it was essential to integrate the fun element into day-to-day thinking.

Quietly, without drama and without appearing that way, MS was a teacher at every opportunity, showing more than telling people what is right and what's not, what is acceptable and what isn't. He was forever approachable. Till such time that he was with the Indian team, his door was open to all and sundry from the time he woke up till it was bedtime. Once he closed it shut at night, that was it; it wouldn't open till the next morning, come hell or high water.

Since he practised detached attachment, MS wasn't fixated on results, which translated to taking failures in the right spirit. No team needs a shellacking at its darkest, most debilitating hour. If MS felt the need for harsh words, he would put them away for a more opportune moment, though he would make a significant statement in the immediacy of a debacle. It's just that he did it subtly and naturally, without stretching the moment out or suggesting that he was haranguing.

That was how MS operated; his style and approach obviously commanded terrific respect, but with respect also came loyalty. And once you are loyal to something, you go to any length to show what you want to do for the team.

MS is a leader par excellence, and he obviously has great tactical acumen. He instinctively knows how to get the best out of any cricketer, and he is a master at managing players on the field. He isn't shy of throwing you into a pressure-cooker situation, but there is a method to the way he goes about it. Especially from a bowler's point of view, MS gives you every opportunity to perform well, but he also makes sure he gives you the ball at the right opportunity.

It is important to make the distinction between opportunity and the quality of opportunity. As a leader, MS never overlooks a player till he has given them enough opportunities with quality. He is extremely wary of writing anyone off because he appreciates the efforts they have put in to reach the national team. There is a long list of cricketers who have benefitted from MS providing the right opportunity with quality. Virat wouldn't have played in the Adelaide Test in 2012 or Rohit wouldn't have opened the batting in one-day cricket in 2013 had MS not pursued his philosophy of qualitative opportunities. That list includes the likes of Ashwin and Jadeja, Ishant and Shami, you can go on and on. To each of them, MS provided the quality of opportunity for them to showcase their skill sets, their ability.

That's a trait that stays with the leader forever. Look at how MS handled Ruturaj Gaikwad during IPL 2020. The youngster took a few games to find his feet, but since MS was convinced of the quality he possessed, he persisted with him without putting him under undue pressure. Look at where Gaikwad is today. That is MS's strength—the trust he shows in the players.

During our tour of England in 2021, Dinesh Karthik and I bumped into Moeen Ali in Leeds during the Test match. We had a freewheeling conversation that veered from one topic to another before settling on Moeen's stint with Chennai Super Kings. It was inevitable that he would be asked to compare the captaincy styles of MS and Eoin Morgan, the England white-ball skipper.

Moeen isn't a diplomat; he is essentially a nice guy but will speak his mind, no matter what. He was all praise for Morgan because like MS, Morgan, too, is a bowlers' captain. 'He's a very quiet person, he doesn't put pressure on the bowler. He has a lot of spirit and is very positive. But MS, he is different, he's something else. Just the way he says things, it gives you so much encouragement and is a feel-good factor.'

The England all-rounder spoke about a game in Mumbai in IPL 2021 where he was being taken to the cleaners on a flat deck. In the middle of the carnage, MS walked up to Moeen and told him, 'It's okay to be hit, there's not much you can do about it. The pitch is just too good. Don't worry if you get hit. but try and concede fours if you can instead of sixes.' As he narrated the story, Moeen's eyes opened wide with astonishment and disbelief. 'The captain is saying, "If you are hit for fours, no problem. Avoid going for sixes." I mean, can you believe it?'

Through that one narrative, Moeen summed up MS perfectly, pithily put his mode of operation into words. How MS brings the loyalty out of a player is a masterclass in the art of leadership—a character trait that made him one of the world's most celebrated, revered, decorated and adored captains.

That is one style of leadership. And then there is Virat's, reiterating that there is no one single way to skin the cat. In terms of win-loss ratio, Virat's record as captain is second to none. He wears his heart on his sleeve and as captain, he showed the team how to embrace pressure. He'd never allow the game to drift, and at practice, he wanted to do the most demanding drills. His motto was that if you prepared for the toughest thing and the easier option came along, nothing like it. But you were ready for the hard yards, as opposed to doing the easy things in practice and being found wanting when it came to the crunch.

Virat brought fearlessness, passion and intensity to his style of leadership. He demanded all these from every player who was part of every team under him. And he demanded excellence when it came to fitness and fielding, both of which are controllables and proactive rather than reactive traits. Because he walked the talk in those aspects, it was inevitable that the rest would fall in line; fitness and fielding became absolute non-negotiables in the Kohli era.

Virat had a clear vision for Indian cricket. The way he took the team forward, especially in the red-ball version, was unprecedented. To him, playing for a draw was like losing a game. His extreme competitiveness meant no matter the situation, he would always be thinking 'win'. There were so many situations when we were down in the dumps and he would say, 'Somehow, if we can conjure another 150 runs, we will win.' And the rest of us would be wondering where the next 50 runs would come from, let alone the next 150.

There was a game in Pallekele on our tour of Sri Lanka in 2017, the second ODI. We were chasing 231 in 47 overs and it was like Akila Dananjaya was celebrating Deepavali, hitting the stumps for fun and lighting up the zing bails. Every few minutes, the bails would start glowing and in no time, we were around 130 for seven, needing 100 runs to win, though the balls remaining was not a factor. Virat himself was bowled for four, and after removing his gear, he came back out to the viewing area to watch the proceedings.

MS and Bhuvi were batting, and out of the blue, Virat said, '*Aur bees run yeh log banayenge toh* (If these people make another 20 runs), we are winning this. *Mahi bhai poora khelenge, nikaal denge match* (Mahi bhai will bat the length of the innings, he will win us the match).' We looked at him stupefied, almost mortified at how simple he made it sound. And guess what? MS and Bhuvi took us home with a century stand.

I am not saying we won because Virat said so, but to me, this was another example of how he's thinking 'win' in any situation. When even one of those situations translates into an amazing victory, his thinking becomes contagious and everyone starts to believe that nothing is impossible. We have seen that happen so many times, especially in Test cricket. Yes, we have fallen short by a country mile more than once, but I haven't come across anyone else who has the belief that no situation can't be overcome, however much the odds might be stacked against you.

One of Virat's greatest contributions to Indian cricket is getting the players to not get caught up in thinking about pitches, about playing away from home. Between him and Ravi, they created a culture where every game was approached like a home game, and where everyone was constantly reminded that the pitch was the same for both teams.

Take the five-bowler theory, for instance. Yes, that gives you the best chance of picking up 20 wickets, but it also means the six batters must accept more responsibility. There is no cushion of an additional specialist batter, so the five full-time batters and the wicketkeeper-batter carried the onus of making the bulk of the runs. That was his way of getting the best out of the batters. He wanted them to be fearless, to embrace the most difficult things that people generally try to steer clear of and be positive and win-minded at all times, think that we are capable of winning every game we played. He made sure his culture came to stay by creating little habits of excellence, especially by himself batting first on the trickiest of pitches at practice. He didn't mind looking ugly in practice if that made things easier for him on match-day. Virat has never been short on self-belief, and that defined his style of leadership more than anything else.

During my time with the Indian team, the other two men who had decent shots at captaincy, if only in a stand-in capacity, were Rohit and Ajinkya. Rohit's leadership mantra was simple; he tried to make everyone a leader. He would go to each bowler and tell him, 'You are the captain. You come sit with me and we'll chalk out a plan. What field do you want? What lines?' He would sit with the analysts. He would sit with the bowlers individually and collectively, and plan intricately.

He would want the bowler to be the captain of the particular over he was sending down. He is a great believer in strategizing and planning and will never take the field without Plans A, B and C. He backed his planning and also backed his bowlers to execute the plans. Rohit would be part of all the meetings. He would listen to other batters, their ideas on the game and how they would like to approach an innings, and he would let them lead their innings without interfering in any significant way.

Rohit was the captain at the Nidahas Trophy in Sri Lanka in March 2018 and the Asia Cup in the UAE in September that year. India famously won both those titles and what struck me was Rohit's tactical acumen. He is highly reliant on data and information, is supremely meticulous and uses data to make his plans. He gives the space every player needs and even when he is the captain, he is still one of the boys.

During my seven years with the Indian side, no tour was more challenging than the one in Australia in 2020–21—without a doubt. If there was any series defined by the man-management and leadership skills of the support staff, this was it. Something was happening every day and we had to take swift decisions. We had to get the boys together, keep them together and make sure they were in the right frame of mind.

And I think that's where Ajinkya truly stood up, the leader in him surfaced brilliantly. After what happened in Adelaide, we would have loved to have Virat all the way through because of his aggression, because he gets under Australia's skin so well. But on the flip side, once he left for India, I feel the Australians thought they had already won the series. We were shattered, Virat was gone, Shami was gone, the series was theirs for the taking, they believed.

That could have been their undoing, but to attribute our success only to that will be far from the truth. What stood out was Ajinkya's calmness, his trust in the plans and his willingness to allow others to have their time under the sun in the last three Tests.

I've often heard the use of the term 'Kohli cam', suggesting that no matter where Virat plays, at least one television camera is constantly trained on him. And why not? It helps the broadcasters; it makes for great drama because you are assured of that with Virat. But Ajinkya doesn't evoke the same emotion. He did exceptionally well in the Melbourne Test, especially, but the camera was not on him all the time.

Ajinkya allowed Siraj to blossom, he allowed Washi to come into his own. He empowered Rishabh and Shubman, he let Ashwin do his own thing, Pujara do his stuff. He gave them space and all but told them, 'You take your time. This is your time, go ahead and enjoy yourself. I'll be behind you; I'll always be behind you.' That reflected Ajinkya's personality perfectly; he was being true to his innate character.

Like MS, Ajinkya also gave the players opportunity with quality. In Siraj's debut Test in Melbourne, Ajinkya brought him on reasonably late on the first day, only after lunch. Siraj wasn't quite there in his first spell, but Ajinkya was patient and brought him back on when the ball started to swing. He kept reminding bowlers about their game plan. He brought with him a calmness and in red-ball cricket, he knew when to push the buttons and when to ease back.

But make no mistake; he was not a weak character. There was this incident when Prithvi was fielding at short leg in a warm-up game in Drummoyne, Sydney. The batter went for a sweep and Prithvi got smacked. As he tried to limp off the park towards the dressing room, Ajinkya was quickly on his case. From his position at slip, he had clearly seen exactly where Prithvi had been hit, which was on the shin pad. Ajinkya went up to him and said firmly, 'Don't take one more step. No one will replace you on the field. I know nothing's wrong with you, I saw the ball hit your shin pad. Maybe you were waiting for an opportunity to go back inside, but that's not happening. Go back to short leg and get into position.' Prithvi knew his bluff had been called and subtly, Ajinkya had told the rest that he would brook no shenanigans. I was mightily relieved as I was the one slated to go in as a substitute as we had only XI for that game.

Ajinkya can be firm when he has to be without being harsh, which is why India have such a good record under him. He has led the team in four Tests against Australia and India have won three of them, including two away from home. That's a fantastic record for someone who doesn't get to captain often, or in a string of games. He understands the game very well. He is very easy-going and approachable, and I got the sense that the senior players feel a greater sense of responsibility when he is the captain; they start chipping in more.

If I had to use one word to describe his style of functioning as captain, I would go for 'inclusive'. Very inclusive. Why, I don't know. Whether it is because he wants more ideas or it is because fewer people convey ideas or it's because he himself is short of ideas, I don't know! Jokes aside, he has been the most democratic captain, if you know where I am coming from.

As is obvious from above, leadership can come in many different ways; every captain will have his own method. Within this set of four captains, the concepts that come to mind are loyalty, fearlessness, team culture, meticulous planning and being inclusive. With Virat, obviously, you get a few other things—the passion and intensity as a leader; the fearlessness he wants to create. Virat is a movement, whereas MS is different. He doesn't just lead a team, he inspires a generation. He literally moved a million kids to play the sport—that is beyond question.

Virat, too, has inspired a generation, but he has also given them an aggressive option. If you want to take that option, you can do so. But his message is clear: 'This is how I've played and led; this is how I have achieved my 68 per cent success rate in different formats of the game. If everyone fears the Indian team now, it's because of our approach as much as our skills. Take it or leave it, that's your call.'

The character of any team is defined by its captain, it has to be. After all, you're only as good as your team. The team has to respond to the leader's call. Virat outlined his vision clearly: 'This is how we're going; this is how we're attacking. We have to stick with it.' But he knew he had the ammunition to do it. He was after Arun, often telling him of a particular bowler, 'Paaji, I want him to bowl like this,' 'I want him to bowl here,' 'I want him to do this,' 'In six months, I want him like this.' That's how his mind worked. To set a good record outside India in Tests, to him, it was always, 'fast bowlers, fast bowlers, fast bowlers, fast bowlers!'

Towards that end, he had an able ally in Arun, who diligently made sure there was always a pool of eight to 10 pacemen available. That process was aided by the other coaches, the IPL and also by a lot of networking. But the process was only made possible because Virat was very clear on what he wanted.

For two years between the start of 2015 and the beginning of 2017, India had two separate captains—while Virat had taken charge of the Test side, MS was still the limited-overs skipper. Virat was still learning the ropes, learning the art of captaincy in that phase, and it helped that he had so much respect for MS. It was MS who made the team and all the players —whether it was Virat himself or Rohit or Ashwin or Jadeja or Bhuvi— acknowledged that fact. They were grateful for the way MS had groomed the team and they were aware of the bond that existed between Virat and MS. Virat was a total MS fan, an MS disciple and has called him his captain for life. None of that was only for public consumption.

Of course, there were two different styles of captaincy, but the team was proficient in terms of shifting seamlessly from one format to another and didn't struggle to comprehend what its character would be in each of those formats. I think that's a great tribute not just to the adaptability of the boys but also to the leadership skills of MS and Virat. We played so many Test matches in that period and our only Test defeat was to Australia in Pune. We had an excellent run in white-ball cricket too, which spilled over when Virat became the limited-overs captain as well at the start of 2017 and we made it to the final of the ICC Champions Trophy.

In those two years, the support staff also had a big part to play in ensuring the transition was smooth and swift. Be it Ravi or Anil Kumble, both were an integral part of the process and ensured that the channels of communication were clear and open. After all, at the end of the day, even if the style of leadership may have been different, the goals were the same. You might take different routes but the destination was the same and the team was mature enough to understand what the goal was. Maybe in that regard, we did luck out!

8

MISSING THE WOOD
FOR THE TREES

'Who is the guy in Afghanistan who is going to bowl so quick tomorrow? We should be practising sweeps and reverse sweeps to unsettle their spinners.'

Making decisions is your pathway to your destiny and the single distinguishing characteristic that separates the good leaders from the great. The leaders that are really outstanding are the ones who are great at making decisions. You don't have to get every decision right; you have to get the majority right. If you can get two-thirds of your decisions right, you are doing really well. Even with the best will in the world, you are just not going to get them all right.[*]

Gareth Southgate, the England football manager, couldn't have said it better. Decision-making is almost as integral to success in any walk of life as one's skills and abilities. During the course of our lives, we are required to make a million decisions, some of which we come to regret; to call them mistakes might be a

---

[*]Gareth Southgate on a live television interview after England's loss in the 2018 World Cup.

little harsh. In the context of Indian cricket during our tenure, there are a few things we could and should have done differently.

No high-performance environment can become so without mistakes being made. When we as coaches or support staff take decisions by the dozens every day, and many of these are taken on the fly under pressure, it is inevitable that some of them will prove wrong in terms of the end results achieved. Many of the decisions we took didn't yield the desired result, though the biggest mistake was something that came about despite the lack of time pressure.

I am referring, of course, to the No. 4 position for the 2019 World Cup, although we had four full years from 2015 to identify and get someone settled at that pivotal spot. No. 4 is such a crucial position in the batting order. He is expected to be the kind of player who takes the baton from the openers, from the top three, and passes it on to the finishers. You need to have someone who can strike at 80–90 per 100 balls for the most part and finishes his innings with a strike rate of 100. It's an acquired skill; it doesn't come naturally to everyone. Unfortunately, we didn't give anyone a chance to settle down, fail and learn. Again, I emphasize, to fail and learn. We wanted results immediately and so if someone failed in two or three games, we moved on to the next guy.

I really have no excuses; we had the same batting coach (Sanjay Bangar) for that entire period, the same fielding coach (yours truly) for the entirety except for the tour of the West Indies in 2016. The head coach (Ravi Shastri) and the bowling coach (Bharat Arun) weren't around for a year when Anil Kumble was in charge. But all told, we had ample time to button down a suitable candidate for that position. To me, in hindsight, the inability to do so was a mistake that was very much controllable; this was a process-driven mistake.

Multiple factors contributed to a blunder that would come back and bite us when it mattered the most. It wasn't until Ravi returned to the set-up in 2017 after a year away that the process of identifying the core group for the World Cup began in right earnest. We realized in Sri Lanka in the middle of that year that we only had about 50 matches before the big event in England.

Plans were made in the bowling department—the need to get the two wrist-spinners (Chahal and Kuldeep) going in the middle overs in the quest for wickets, about Bumrah and Bhuvi being the main pacers, and how we wanted Hardik to get more batting exposure towards the last third of the innings because he fits like a glove at that position and gives us the balance we require as he can give us a fair few overs, too.

But nothing was spoken about the No. 4 position; it was all but taken for granted. That is just a very poor look, with the benefit of hindsight. We missed a major trick and that did us in the end as far as the tournament was concerned.

Looking back, it's staggering that between the tour of Sri Lanka in August–September 2017 and the start of our World Cup campaign in June 2019, we played 10 different batters at the No. 4 position in 49 games. Except Ambati Rayudu, no one played more than seven games in that slot. At home against Sri Lanka in December 2018, MS and Dinesh Karthik batted at two-down; when we went to South Africa in early January, Ajinkya Rahane batted there for the entire series. In England that summer, it was K.L. Rahul. I can see where we messed up.

At the risk of sounding like I am making up an excuse, the period between the two World Cups in 2015 and 2019 was when Virat became the de facto No. 4 in the sense of building on the platform the openers provided and batting through the innings, allowing the finishers to come in and do their thing. Virat was unreal in those four years. Batting first or chasing, he was adept at finishing off innings nine times out of 10, be it for helping us to a massive total or scaling down whatever the opposition posted. I had a quick look at the staggering numbers. In 69 innings, he amassed 4,306 runs at the incredible average of 78.29 and a phenomenal strike rate of 98.33. He made 19 centuries and 16 half-centuries, which translates to a 50-plus knock every second innings. Oh no, I am not blaming Virat for us overlooking the No. 4 slot, don't get me wrong. But did his extraordinary run contribute to that process in some oblique way? Perhaps it did.

I agree that was out of character for a support group which got a lot of other things right. I mean, we are talking about Ravi, Sanjay, Arun, Virat and myself—it was a shocker from us. We were unsuccessful in giving anyone the confidence to grow into that position, and it was no surprise that when it mattered the most, we were found wanting. We missed it, plain and simple.

Perhaps we got carried away by the fact that we had a gun top-three—Rohit Sharma, Shikhar Dhawan and Virat Kohli— and two exceptional finishers in MS and Hardik, and therefore overlooked the significance of No. 4. It sounds simplistic enough, but how could we have let that happen, no matter how prolific these five batters were in their respective positions?

I have heard theories that the No. 4 position wasn't a factor at the World Cup except at the semifinal. Correct, but that's because in all the other games, at least one, if not two, of the top-three batted deep into the innings. We were never tested; we didn't suffer a meltdown until the New Zealand game. And when push came to shove, we couldn't respond. I know it's not my place to say so, but there is a lesson in it for think tanks going forward. I can say with reasonable confidence that I don't see Rohit and Rahul Dravid making the same mistake.

We didn't have a left-hander in the middle-order either. We did veer towards Rishabh, who came to the West Indies in 2017 on what was his first oversees tour with the senior Indian men's cricket team, but he didn't play a single game. Subsequently, he got runs in the IPL and worked his way back into the team. Ravi was a big fan of Rishabh and his ability to turn games in a short time, but some of his teammates were not big fans of his work ethic at that point. Of course, later on, the kid changed his ways and we did bring him into the fold when Shikhar got injured at the World Cup, but by the time he got his first hit in the competition, half the tournament was over.

As a group of support staff and coaches, if we had to do things all over again, this is one of the first things we would like to correct—our approach towards the No. 4 position. And I'd like to think I'd be more proactive and advocate the case of Shreyas Iyer, get him to play more and get him ready for the World Cup. Needless to say, life doesn't accord such luxuries.

One of the biggest disappointments during our tenure was that we couldn't win an ICC trophy. We had six bites at the cherry, including the WTC final. The five white-ball competitions were the 2015 and 2019 50-over World Cups, the 2017 Champions Trophy and the 2016 and 2021 T20 World Cups.

Let's take the WTC. Our consistency throughout the league phase allowed us to finish on top of the standings and qualify for the final. New Zealand played better than us in Southampton in conditions that they were far more familiar with than us. That's not an excuse, just a statement of fact. I didn't think there was any shame in finishing runners-up, much as we would have loved to be crowned the inaugural World Test Champions. Everyone knows the odds we had to overcome, particularly in Australia in 2020–21, to make it to the title round. More than a disappointment, I'd look at it as a fantastic, brilliant run.

As far as the limited-overs tournaments are concerned, there were no flaws in our processes except at the 2019 World Cup and our inexplicable ignorance of the No. 4 position. Yes, you could argue that there weren't enough left-handers in the top six, but that's alright. Would we have loved one more left-hander apart from Shikhar? For sure. Was that a game-changer? I don't think so.

We were perhaps a little undone by the rain and the conditions on the reserve day in the semifinal against New Zealand, but that's only because I am being a little defensive and looking for crumbs. With our batting line-up and the form we had shown all through the tournament, there is no excuse for not scaling down 240, no matter how well New Zealand exploited the two new balls. Even on the reserve day, we had bowled four brilliant overs; Jadeja took an exceptional catch and effected a stunning run out, so we took plenty of momentum into the innings break. But we then imploded in the first 45 minutes of our chase, and that was that.

There were a fair few tactical flaws in some of the other competitions. Take the Champions Trophy in 2017, for instance. We had had an excellent campaign leading up to the final against Pakistan, whom we had brushed aside in our first game of the competition. We had won batting first and were confident enough that our surprise loss to Sri Lanka was no more than an aberration that we had set right in subsequent encounters.

The final was at The Oval, a rerun of our first match on one of the best batting tracks I have come across in international cricket. The outfield was lightning quick; the ground wasn't the biggest. The general consensus was that should we win the toss, we should bat first, pile up the runs and allow scoreboard pressure to work on Pakistan. Agreed, by then we had graduated into excellent chasers, but the value of runs on the board in a cup final can't be overstated.

For reasons best known to him and fairly so, Virat decided that we would be better off chasing. To compound matters, Bumrah dismissed Fakhar Zaman off a no ball and we were punished for that indiscretion. Zaman made a flowing century. Pakistan pulled away to 338 for four and we had our worst batting day of the Champions Trophy to be beaten by a country mile.

As we were sliding to a heavy defeat, I couldn't help but cast my mind back a year and a quarter to the semifinals of the T20 World Cup at the Wankhede Stadium in Mumbai. In conditions similar to what existed at The Oval, we only posted

192 for two against the mighty West Indies. I say 'only' because I felt we should have posted at least 220, we were 25 runs short of what I thought was par for the course in the context of the game. Where we should have been hitting fours and sixes, we were content with running ones and twos. During the duration of our innings, we had only 17 fours and four sixes, which certainly didn't reflect the deck on which we were playing. Again, like at The Oval, we dismissed batters off no balls—twice, lest we should forget—and went down quite tamely. Just for the record, West Indies smashed 20 fours and Lendl Simmons alone struck more sixes in 51 deliveries than we all did in 120.

We didn't read the Mumbai deck to perfection. We didn't account for the dew; we didn't make allowances for the fact that we would need the cushion of a few extra runs while defending a target for these same reasons. We made a few tactical errors, as we did in the Champions Trophy final the following year.

Our campaign at the T20 World Cup in 2021 ended even before it began. When we entered the bubble and once players from various IPL franchises checked it, it was obvious they were jaded mentally and physically. To have finished a tournament as intense as the IPL just 10 days before the start of our World Cup campaign was far from ideal. As the draw would have it, we ran into the two toughest opponents in our group right at the beginning. Once we lost Rohit and KL to Shaheen Afridi, the Pakistan game unravelled quickly. We traded punches briefly against New Zealand before fatigue got in the way and we couldn't sustain our intensity. I understand it was a freak occurrence that year, with the IPL postponed halfway through due to the second wave of the pandemic, but going forward, I think it won't be a bad practice to ensure that our players are fresh and well-prepared heading into a competition of the magnitude of a World Cup because even at full tilt, the challenges and pressures of such tournaments are myriad and immense.

Another area where we could have been better is in creating more security for the players. In the months since my time with the Indian team ended, I have sought out several players to understand if my earlier concerns were justified or unfounded, and I realized that there had been a little bit of insecurity within the set-up. There has always been talk of building a good team culture and giving more security to players, so that the team environment is good and the player is not worried about his place, which in turn would ensure he performs better. But you pit that against the fact that you are in the business of winning, you have got a billion people who only want to see you win and they can't take you losing.

Consequently, only the guys who are in form will represent the country because every match is about winning. You have to perform that balancing act, which is delicate and tricky. This is not a development squad where you say I have this set of 15 guys, only this 15 will play the entire year; we will keep rotating and we will build on that, no matter the results. We couldn't afford to do that. We had to go clearly by form—who is good enough in that particular moment, in the best mindset, in the best form; who can perform for India. Also, sometimes in international cricket, match-ups are big. Against a certain team, if a certain player is not a match-up, although he is good player or has been doing well, we may have to make a change to win that game. Somewhere, we were unable to do that balancing act of giving security and keeping the winning percentage going. We as support staff are very proud of our winning percentage—close to 70 per cent. In international cricket, if you have such numbers, it is a big tick, a big pass. Given that we had a team with that kind of a winning percentage, the balancing act could have been better. But I don't know how. If you ask me if I would have done anything differently towards that end, I wouldn't have an answer because it is very difficult for coaches to get their balancing act right all the time. You have to answer sponsors; you have to answer broadcasters;

you have to answer administrators. At the end of the day, you are ultimately judged on the results alone.

It's inevitable that the perception will linger from the outside that there were different strokes for different folks. That perception was perhaps strengthened by how hard we tried to ensure Hardik was available for selection, if only as a batter, because there was no replacement for him, there was nobody half as good in terms of skill sets for the T20 World Cup in 2021.

Hardik was the answer to our prayers for a medium-paced all-rounder. He was sharp and could rev it up to 140. He swung the ball in helpful conditions. He wasn't shy of testing out the bounce of the pitch and had the happy knack of getting wickets. But first and foremost, he was a fabulous ball-striker, free-flowing and effortless; his lithe frame belying his power and the penchant to hit a long ball.

Once he got injured in the Asia Cup in 2018, he wasn't the same cricketer. Yes, he came back for the World Cup the next year and bowled well in most matches, but we were apprehensive of a breakdown at all times. Even so, we kept the faith in him as a pure batter because of the untold damage he is capable of towards the back end of an innings. That move seemed vindicated when he adapted superbly to playing as a specialist batter in the white-ball leg on the Australia tour in 2020–21.

When ahead of the T20 World Cup in 2021 we came to know that Hardik was unlikely to be more than a bit player, at best, with the ball, we had a big decision to make. Numbers suggested that between overs 14 and 20, he was one of the top active run getters for the country, at an excellent strike rate. That tipped the scales in his favour as opposed to someone like Shreyas, who hadn't played cricket for a while due to an injury and who, in any case, was seen as a top-order batter in T20 cricket. He wasn't viewed as someone who could come in at No. 5 or 6 and smash 30 runs from 15 balls, for instance.

Even though Hardik couldn't bowl, he was the only guy available who could do that, who had done that, and who had reasonable experience of the pulls and pressures of big tournaments. No one else was capable of the impact he could make when he walked in around the fourteenth over. It's another matter that he didn't get going, but that was the reasoning behind his inclusion despite our knowledge that he would at best have a marginal role as a bowler. I believe one of the reasons he couldn't deliver is that he is just not the kind of guy who was comfortable in a bubble, that was just not him.

I have an issue with batters not bowling these days, and this was something I discussed with MS, too, during the World Cup. One of the main reasons for that is our coaching system. With the Indian team now, as it has been for a little while, we have three dedicated throwdown specialists and generally we get four nets. Two nets are used for full-fledged bowling; in the other two nets, there is always someone who wants extra batting. Most of the batters finish their 20–25 minutes of batting, after which there are between three and five men waiting with weapons in their hand—I am referring, of course, to the sidearm or the slinger.

When they finish their stints against the bowlers, all the batters go over and bat for between 45 minutes and an hour against these slingers. After that, if they still have the energy, they take some catches and are done for the session.

Contrast this against the olden days where there were no slingers. Consequently, once you finished batting, you had to take care of your teammates. If there was no one to bowl to the lower order, you had to go and bowl to them in the nets; you couldn't just bat and walk away. That's why in the early 2000s, we had so many top-order batters who were more than competent bowlers: Sachin Tendulkar, Virender Sehwag, Sourav Ganguly and Yuvraj Singh. That's something we need to look into. Across formats, all our batters only bat, they don't bowl at all.

Sticking with the T20 World Cup of 2021, I am afraid we played primitive and conservative cricket. How many reverse sweeps, for instance, did our batters attempt? Was there any creativity in the shot making? Nothing that I can remember. In the first two matches against Pakistan and New Zealand, we didn't show enough resolve and steel to play those strokes, whereas in the last three games, there was no need for such shots. There was no innovation to our batting at the World Cup. We didn't have too many capable of playing that way. All our hitting was restricted to either mid-wicket or the straight field.

Nowadays, you find innovators even in street cricket. The system must change; you have to produce more creative cricketers and clearly, the starting point can't be after you make the national team. That has to start from the grassroots level. You must start teaching it to 14-year-olds. We need to incorporate creativity in our coaching. What gets rewarded gets repeated, simple. If you don't reward for creativity, if you didn't allow young players to experiment and make mistakes, if you don't create an environment where mistakes are admitted, accepted and used as a tool to improve, neither you will instill security nor will you make creative players. We failed to do that; as a group, we didn't do that. How many creative batters have played for us in the last five years? All our hitters are straight. We practise so much and because of that, our batting is so good. I know I said the slingers don't help in creating bowlers, but it's also because of the slingers that our batting is superb. But this is the flip side I am talking about.

While batting in the nets, some of our batters scooped or reversed, but I didn't see anyone practising it specifically, of which I am a big fan. I have worked with Glenn Maxwell as well as a lot of other overseas cricketers. When they practise such strokes after their designated batting stint, I am thrilled.

Just to put things in perspective. We were at an optional practice session at the ICC Academy before the Afghanistan game in the T20 World Cup. Only three or four batters turned up, and they were playing against our slingers, who were going 140–150 kmph. I asked MS, 'Who is the guy in Afghanistan who is going to bowl so quick tomorrow? Can we bring more specificity to our preparations? We should be practising sweeps and reverse sweeps to unsettle their spinners.' I took Suryakumar Yadav, who was returning from back spasm, into a net and made him play a few sweeps, but I didn't tell that to the others. It was not my style of coaching. I pacified myself thinking that players know best how to ready themselves for a game. I did tell Ravi that if they want, I was ready to bowl to them because against their spinners, all we needed to do was sweep, sweep and sweep. That's how you put them off. The following day, guess what shot Rohit employed when he faced Rashid Khan's first bowl.

From a bowler's point of view, if someone sweeps me, I am in trouble. I don't know what to bowl. With the sweep, the batter will manipulate your fields; he will manipulate your line. If someone keeps hitting me straight, I feel okay, but if someone sweeps me, it puts me off. Ask any spinner and I am sure they will say the same thing. Take even someone as accomplished as Ashwin. If you sweep him, he gets frustrated and annoyed.

You can only sweep a good ball, which pitches on a good length or just short of it. Those are the kinds of balls that, if you lunge towards, they can pop into the hands of short-leg or silly point after hitting the edge of the bat or taking the glove. That's the ball you will try to sweep. I feel it is a terrific shot to have. Today, the way cricket is going, the paddle sweep, getting on your knees and scooping—that's definitely the way to go.

I guess the other elephant in the room we must address is the treatment of Ashwin when we played Test cricket overseas. In my view, he is easily the best spinner of his generation, and you don't even need to invoke his numbers to drive that point home. He is crafty and guileful, but what I found most endearing and awe-inspiring was his constant endeavour to better his skills on a daily basis. There is not a single defensive bone in his body, and he holds the view that if you don't work towards improvement, you might as well stop playing.

For a long time, he was our unquestioned No. 1 spinner overseas, but that started changing in the middle of 2018, by which time we had decided that on away tours, unless the conditions so dictated, we would often play only one spinner to complement our exceptional pace attack. Even so, Ashwin started in South Africa and in England, where he bowled quite beautifully in the first Test in Birmingham when he picked up seven wickets in the match.

I was convinced that was the kind of performance he needed to step up and emphatically silence those who held his away record against him. In my book, Ashwin has been arguably India's number one match-winner in Test cricket for a large part of the decade spanning from 2011 to 2020. One might say that the status should belong to Virat, with which I agree to a large extent, but how can you argue with Ashwin's five Test hundreds, 30 five-wicket hauls and seven 10-wicket hauls? And to top it up, he has got 'Player of the Series' on nine occasions. I will be honest and admit that Ashwin did not quite get the status he deserved as the number one match-winner of the team.

As that England tour unravelled, so did Ashwin the bowler, unfortunately. He picked up a hip strain and, therefore, was unable to complete his action, which meant he wasn't able to put enough body into his bowling. In the next two Tests at Lord's and in Nottingham, he picked up just one wicket and by the time we went to Southampton for the fourth Test, the old bogey of Ashwin's performances overseas and his fitness reared its head again.

I am not sure Ashwin was 100 per cent fit for the Southampton Test. It was the game in which Moeen Ali took nine wickets by hitting the rough and getting enough purchase from there, but Ashwin was so injured that he was unable to put the ball in the rough. Should he not have been picked? He said he was fit and as a senior player, he, therefore, had the trust of the team management. I don't know, maybe he felt he was ready for five days at the start of the match, but as the Test progressed, perhaps the injury worsened and he couldn't function at his optimum. What happened with him is still a mystery to me, but I think that game is where he lost his status as India's No. 1 spinner overseas.

Lest anyone should get the wrong impression, I am not trying to hold Ashwin responsible for our defeat in Southampton. It's very wrong to point a finger at one person for any loss in a team game. Maybe we depended too much on him in that game and he couldn't come up trumps because of his injury. In some ways, Ashwin was a victim of his own standards.

When we went to Australia later that year, Ashwin had won the think tank over with his excellent bowling against West Indies at home, in India. We didn't get swayed by the fact that he got nine wickets in two Tests; the ball was leaving his hand beautifully and he was the obvious choice for the Adelaide Test, where he played a massive role in our victory, with six wickets and handy contributions with the bat.

However, he then got injured again (abdominal strain) and didn't play a game subsequently. Having told us that he was fit to play in the final game in Sydney, he pulled out minutes before the toss, which was the sensible thing to do because no one wanted a repeat of Southampton.

We didn't play an overseas Test for another year. Ashwin did have a pretty decent game in Wellington, but it was becoming increasingly difficult to overlook Jadeja's credentials. His batting had come on tremendously. He had done well with the ball whenever he got an opportunity and we couldn't afford to not optimize his all-round skills. Jadeja gave us the balance, batting at No. 7, still allowing us to play four fast bowlers and adding a new dimension with his fielding, which alone was good enough to earn him a place in the XI.

Virat's logic was that when we went to places like New Zealand, where there was 16mm grass on the pitch, he needed just 10 overs or so from his spinner, more in a defensive, holding role and to allow the quicks to operate in short, sharp bursts. It was, therefore, decided that we would go for the better package if the spinner was to have a limited role in his primary craft. Perhaps it was unfair on Ashwin, but that was the thinking of the brains trust.

By the time we returned to Australia towards the end of 2020, it was clear that unless we played two spinners abroad, Ashwin would have to bide his time. But if he was affected by that, there were no signs. At the quarantine camp in Blacktown, Ashwin's presence went unacknowledged for the first three days until Arun decided enough was enough. He told Ravi, 'Ash is bowling outstandingly in the nets. All that's needed is for you to go and give him confidence…make him feel wanted. Put your arm around his shoulder and talk to him, he is your match-winner.'

Ravi saw the wisdom in Arun's words. He is, of course, a master at pumping the lads up and you could see what a massive impact the conversation had on Ashwin. By then, it was clear that Ashwin had worked extremely hard on his fitness, too. He passed all the fitness tests in Blacktown with flying colours. We had to somehow find a way to fit him into our plans, but how?

As destiny would have it, Jadeja got injured during the T20I in Canberra, a hamstring strain followed by a concussion. Ashwin would have his time in the sun, again.

Even in Blacktown, you could see that the ball was just bursting through from his hand. He was bowling like a sock, it was unbelievable. I thought I had seen the best of Ashwin, but this was bowling at a different level. He was just brilliant in Adelaide and had Steve Smith's number in the first two Tests. In Melbourne, Ajinkya brought him on in the first session to exploit the moisture in the track and Ashwin responded like only he can; he killed it.

Ashwin didn't have a great game with the ball in Sydney, but boy, did he bat! His batting had dipped dramatically since the middle of 2017, but this was just a phenomenal effort on the final day. He and Vihari were unremovable. Vihari had done his hamstring; Ashwin's back was gone. In fact, once it became clear that Ashwin would have to go out to bat at some stage, he stood the entire time. He knew if he sat down, it would be impossible for him to get up again. So, he stood in the dressing room for an hour and he stood out in the middle for more than three hours, negotiating everything Australia threw at him as he and Vihari earned us a terrific draw.

By Melbourne, Jadeja had made a full recovery and Ravi decided that we needed to strengthen the bowling. It's not something that usually happens in Indian cricket. When batters fail, it's often the bowlers who are dropped. However, despite being bowled out for 36 in Adelaide, Ravi felt India had the batting to take on Australia. Our focus was on winning the series, for which we needed 20 wickets. We had gone into Adelaide with four bowlers, partly because it was a day-night Test and partly because Jadeja was not available. But once we could summon both our spinners, Ravi made it clear that we would go to Melbourne with all guns blazing, with a positive mindset. The eight-wicket win vindicated that decision.

With such decision-making, you run the risk of losing the odd match. But in that series against Australia, it worked out beautifully. We played one of the greatest series of all time. When Virat left after Adelaide, he was actually replaced in the XI by Jadeja. Who would have imagined that? After we won that Test, we realized we should go in with our five best bowlers overseas and not be fixated on four quicks and a lone spinner.

That's what we did at the WTC final in Southampton, where Ashwin bowled quite beautifully. But by the time we turned up in Nottingham for the first Test against England, we changed our thinking and went back to playing just one spinner. Were we indecisive and confused and quick to pull the trigger? I am not sure. But were we inconsistent in our combinations? Definitely yes.

We were confronted with a green strip in Nottingham, which forced us to refocus on playing four fast bowlers. So, Ashwin or Jadeja? It wasn't an easy call to make, but eventually we went with the latter for several reasons. One is the package I have referred to earlier—what he brings with the ball, with the bat and in the field. The other was the number of left-handers in the English top-order.

That might sound like a contradiction, given Ashwin's stunning record against left-handers. But it's important to remember that unlike New Zealand at the WTC final who had Trent Boult and Neil Wagner, there were no left-arm seamers in either side who could create the rough that would bring Ashwin into play. By contrast, the rough created by the right-arm pacemen would play into Jadeja's hands when he bowled to left-handed batters and turned the ball in from outside off. That meant Jadeja would be a more potent threat than Ashwin on days four and five if the match went that long.

I personally feel Ashwin could have played in the fourth Test at The Oval. On the morning of the game, Ravi and Arun suggested to Virat that both Jadeja and Ashwin play, but the skipper was quite clear that he wanted a 4-1 combination and that Jadeja bowling into the rough would be a factor. Jadeja bashed the ball into the rough so hard that it suddenly started reversing in England's second innings too. So again, the ends justified the means.

It's undeniable that Ashwin played far fewer matches away

from home than he should have. He sat out all four Tests against England, but the way he handled it was unbelievable. He was in excellent space because his family was there. His work ethic and attitude towards the team was exemplary. I am not saying he wasn't gutted, but looking at him, you wouldn't have guessed. He knew the thought process of the team management and considered it to be fair. He didn't worry too much, he was reconciled to the fact that he could only play abroad if we played two spinners, though I know for a fact that he was very hurt after The Oval snub when conditions almost cried out for two spinners of the quality of Ashwin and Jadeja.

Also in hindsight, once we brought Ashwin back into the T20 set-up after nearly five years, we should have straightaway played him against Pakistan and New Zealand in the World Cup. We took a punt on Varun Chakravarthy's 'mystery' and it was a gamble that misfired. Ashwin subsequently showed us the folly of our decision-making.

It's been a long and exhaustive list of failures, if you want— exacerbated by the fractious relationship with the Indian media, for no reason, in my humble opinion.

In 2015, when we travelled to Sri Lanka, Ravi took the initiative of organizing a luncheon get-together involving the support staff and the travelling media. Virat joined us briefly. We went to great lengths to share space and information and I thought this is exactly how it should be. We have a job to do and the media has a job to do, but that didn't mean there shouldn't be some kind of openness and transparency. Ravi himself had been a media man, so he understood the importance of the media's role.

After 2017, however, things took a turn for the worse. I don't know why, but there was a massive sense of distrust, even angst, when it came to the media. I felt the in-house dissection of every press conference and the subsequent outpouring of vitriol in the dressing room or the team bus was a little over the top. I genuinely feel there was no reason for some people in the management group to be cussed about the media, especially after our initial attempts to strike a pleasant working relationship had helped create a healthy atmosphere.

9

CRICKET DURING COVID-19
(Part One)

'No, no, you can't come in. You can't enter the elevator.
We have been told that we must not share the elevator with anyone
from the Indian contingent.'

We were in New Zealand in the first quarter of 2020 when we first heard of Covid-19 and the coronavirus. Truth to tell, we didn't pay much attention. After a superb start to the multi-format tour by sweeping the Kiwis 5-0 in the T20 series, we had our fair share of on-field travails, surrendering the ODI series 0-3. Our energies were concentrated on the two Tests that were to round off the tour, though we couldn't marry desire and ambition with performances, and lost both Tests quite comfortably.

We returned to India in the first week of March, just in time to avoid being stranded in an alien land as the pandemic swept through the world. It was a period of fear and uncertainty. As the positive cases began to stack up globally, India went into a six-week lockdown, forcing not just sport but the entire nation to hunker down and bide time.

Towards the end of May, a few weeks after the lockdown had

been lifted, the support staff got in touch to make tentative plans on how to go about bringing the players back into practice. We discussed sending trainers to different zones, so that contracted players could assemble in one city in each zone through a safe transfer process and work on their fitness in a sanitized bubble. The thinking was that once they worked on their fitness, which was bound to have suffered owing to the long period during which they had no access to training facilities, we would give them enough time to rest and recover before focussing on the skills ahead of our Australia tour in November, for three ODIs, as many T20Is and four Test matches.

Then, the BCCI announced that the delayed IPL would be staged in the UAE from 19 September. Initially, we had planned to have a camp in Ahmedabad for about two weeks before the players left for the UAE and sent those plans across for the BCCI's approval. We, however, noticed that there was a lot of reluctance on the part of the players themselves, who were keen to join their IPL teams instead. The franchises wanted their players to go to the UAE either in late July or early August because they felt they needed four weeks to get back into shape, prepare and gel as a unit.

As it is, we were a little conflicted about what the focus of the camp ought to be—should it be red- or white-ball centric? Should we focus on the Australia tour, or on the IPL? The biggest challenge was that if we managed to get the BCCI's nod for the camp, there was every possibility that the players would constantly be thinking about the IPL, which would be counterproductive to our objectives. Thus, it was decided that we would do away with the idea of a camp and rather have the players training with their franchises.

The BCCI's Sports Science and Sports Medicine (SSSM) team was then tasked with monitoring the fitness of the players. We got all the physios and trainers of the eight franchises and the

SSSM team together, so that the latter could keep a tab on the progress of the players potentially in line to travel to Australia. When the players are with their respective franchises, they are not under our control and therefore we can't directly monitor them. But we wanted to get them back to the optimum best possible because then, we would have less work to do on them from a physical perspective before the marquee Australian series, which was certain to be a humdinger with Steve Smith and David Warner back in the fray.

The SSSM team went to the UAE and put together a plan to work in tandem with the sports science teams of the respective franchises. Most of the players in the three squads for Australia were already in the UAE. Those who weren't playing in the IPL and us members of the support staff then reached Dubai to complete our mandatory quarantine before we all could move into the bubble, which would be in effect from that point to the time we returned to India, more than two-and-a-half months later.

We had little clarity about what to expect when we reached Australia. All we knew was that Cricket Australia (CA) wanted us to quarantine for 14 days on both sides of our travel. That's 28 days cooped up in a room, split only by the long flight from Dubai to Sydney. What this meant was that once we came out of our two-week quarantine in Sydney, we would have only two or three days of practice before the first ODI, on 27 November. After all, the earliest we could leave Dubai was on 11 November, the day after the final of the IPL.

Confusion was a constant companion till we flew out of Dubai. Initially, we were supposed to land in Perth, but the Western Australian government shot that plan down. Then, our touchdown point shifted to Adelaide, but a few days before we were to leave, the cases mounted in South Australia and so Adelaide too was a no go. Brisbane came into the picture because New Zealand Women were engaged in battle with Australia Women. Queensland state rules necessitated that if we landed in Brisbane, we had to undergo 14 days of hard quarantine because there was no way they were allowing us 'soft' quarantine.

We were very clear that 14 days of hard quarantine wasn't acceptable to us. We were game to be in hard quarantine for three days but were keen that after two successive negative tests each, we should be allowed to practise in a safe environment. Finally, the premier of New South Wales, Gladys Berejiklian, obliged, and its government, in collaboration with the Australian Federal Police and the CA, arrived at a solution.

The CA told us that there was a facility in Blacktown, a suburb in Sydney, which had two grounds where we could practise after three days of hard quarantine. That's exactly what we wanted, so we gladly lapped up the offer. But if we thought we were done with the pre-departure drama, we were in for a rude shock.

Three days before we were scheduled to fly out of Dubai, the CA threw a bomb. We were informed that the families of the players and of the coaching and support staff would not be able to enter Australia. This was a curveball because all along, they had maintained that families were allowed, which is why more than half-a-dozen players had called their families over to Dubai, so that they could quarantine for two weeks. This latest missive from the Australian board left us deeply disturbed, and not only because it was completely unexpected.

When we sought the rationale behind the change in the Australian mindset with regard to families travelling, we were told that there were close to 90,000 Aussies stranded abroad due to the pandemic and subsequent travel restrictions, and getting them back home was the Aussie government's main priority. We were also informed that families did not fall under the 'essential workers' category, so the Australians would not issue them a visa.

Confronted with his first major challenge even before the tour began, Ravi put his foot down. He said if the families were not allowed entry, the team would not travel to Australia. 'Do what you want,' was his underlying threat. Ravi didn't engage directly with the CA, instead he passed on his and the contingent's sentiments to the BCCI and left it to the two cricket boards to sort out the issue.

Given the uncertainty, there was a lot of tension within our camp. We understood why the Australian government wanted to get its citizens back home at the earliest and empathized with them. But we couldn't comprehend why that meant our families should not travel. We were flying on a chartered aircraft, so we were not taking up anyone else's seats. And for our players to be in a good space mentally and give their best on the field, they needed their families around. Otherwise, they would be worried about their near and dear ones back in India. If, God forbid, something happened to someone back home and the player had to return to India, he would not be able to come back to Australia.

It was a weekend, and a lot happened over the two days. The BCCI worked overtime, mixing charm offensive with its persuasion skills. Eventually, late on Monday afternoon, permission was secured for players to be accompanied by their families. It was a big relief, more than anything else, for those of us who were unsure of what life in a very tight bubble entailed. Thus, it was then that a huge contingent left from Dubai for Sydney on 12 November 2020, by an Emirates chartered flight. The passengers consisted of our squad and family members, Australian players and coaching and support staff who had been a part of the IPL, officials, commentators, just about anyone headed to Australia back from the IPL and/or for our tour.

Our first taste of what lay ahead came when we arrived in Sydney. It took us two hours to complete all formalities and get out of the airport, from where we were whisked away to the Olympic Park. We were to stay at the Pullman Hotel, and I am not exaggerating when I say that at least my room was hardly bigger than a box—a box that would be my home for the next 14 days. You could look out into nothingness through the only glass window in the room, but, of course, you couldn't open it. And a federal cop was posted on each floor to ensure that all quarantine regulations were adhered to without compromise.

The first three days of hard quarantine were interesting. The hotel had tied up with an Indian restaurant chain called Urban Tadka, from where we could order breakfast, lunch and dinner, which would be delivered at our doorstep. We were told we had to wait at least five minutes after the hotel staff rang the bell before we could open the door. One evening, after dinner, I had left the door ajar, so that I could get rid of the smell of food in the room. Within a minute, I received a call from the reception urging me to shut the door at once. Big brother sure was watching!

Clearly, no housekeeping staff would be entering any of the rooms for the duration of our stay, so there was no question of the bed being made, the linens and towels being changed, and the washroom being cleaned. You had to do everything on your own. There was an adequate supply of detergent and brushes if you wanted to clean the pot, and a few extra towels and an additional set of linen. There was, however, provision for laundry. Every room was provided with a reasonable number of laundry bags. We had to write our names on the tags and leave the bag outside the room, which would only be collected two days later and delivered a further 24 hours thereafter. Effectively, if you left the laundry outside your door on day one, you'd get it back only on day four.

When we reached Sydney, it was without one of the key members of our support staff. Raghu is more than a throwdown specialist, he is the heartbeat of the side. He does everything that is asked of him and more with a beaming smile 24/7/365. He had tested positive for Covid-19 in Bengaluru, and couldn't join us as scheduled in Dubai. Once he had tested negative after 14 days of quarantine in Bengaluru, he took a commercial flight and so couldn't link up with the team immediately. After 14 days of quarantine in a government facility in Sydney, a Covid-19 test picked up some dead cells in his sample and so the test result was deemed inconclusive. Since he hadn't returned a negative test, he was forced to stay in isolation for 14 more days. In effect, the poor guy spent 42 days in quarantine. There was some discussion on whether or not he should join the team, but Ravi was insistent that no matter when, Raghu had to be with the side; there was no two ways about it.

After three days of hard quarantine and all of us testing negative twice each, we were allowed to start practising. We had a contingent of 32 or 33 players, including net bowlers. Unfortunately, two of the four net bowlers—Varun Chakravarthy and Kamlesh Nagarkoti—didn't even make the trip to Australia, getting injured at practice in Dubai. We were left with just two net bowlers, Ishan Porel and T. Natarajan, who quickly began to be called 'Netarajan' (a pun on his name)!

I must admit, the practice facility at Blacktown was excellent. There were two beautiful grounds with floodlights, gyms, dressing rooms and a fantastic practice area. You couldn't have asked for anything more. The pitches weren't necessarily of the highest quality, but we weren't complaining. Three days into practice, Porel did his knee and was in no position to bowl any further, so he flew back home, leaving us with Netarajan as the sole surviving net bowler. Netarajan has a good strong engine and his rural background meant he had put in the tough yards.

Our practice sessions were divided into two hours on the white ball and two hours on the red and pink balls, with the multi-format players given the option of making their own choices. For the first six days, Virat practised exclusively against the pink ball because he would only be playing the day-night opening

Adelaide Test and missing the remaining Tests. For the last few days, he shifted into white-ball mode, reiterating how focussed he is in his preparation when it comes to Test cricket.

I lugged three bowling bags around, digging into them depending on which group turned up for a fielding session. For the first two hours, when the white-ball team was working on its skills, the red-ball group would be in the gym or engaged in running, conditioning and strengthening. After a half-hour break, the groups would swap places. This was pretty much the routine for the first three days, at the end of which both batting coach Vikram Rathour and I were running on empty. Like the rest of the guys, the batting coach and I were also coming off a long layoff, and we had been working nonstop, without even a semblance of a break. Every muscle and every bone in the body ached; we were sore and stiff, suffering from DOMS (delayed onset muscle soreness), also known as 'muscle fever'.

We had no option but to soldier through the aches and pains. After three days of hard practice and nets, we had open nets or centre-wicket practice. On days five and six, there was match simulation, with one half of the ground cordoned off. We had a set of two bowlers bowling 10 overs to two batters, who were given targets. For white-ball players, it was 60 runs, with the batters docked 10 runs each time they were dismissed. We made this a competition, batters vs bowlers, and gave different batters different scenarios depending on what they might encounter in the games. For Test simulation, we would ask Virat and Pujara to bat from 10 for two; we'd have separate targets for the openers, for Nos. 5 and 6. We had two excellent days of very good match simulations.

Gradually, we got the players going with regard to fielding and catching. We started with tennis balls and soft balls, focussing on hand-eye coordination drills—some fun, some games. By the second day of hard practice, the boys were regaining their core skills and by the time we got to the open nets, they were taking slip catches with the hard cricket ball. I could sense excitement building slowly within the set-up. The interest levels were high and the vibes very positive. But we didn't want to end up doing too much too soon, so after day six came our first break.

At Blacktown, we couldn't enter the ground when the curators were working on the pitches, on the outfield. Only after they left the premises were we allowed to step on the ground. If they had to come in to draw the crease in the middle of our practice session, we had to all go huddle in the dressing room and wait for them to finish. It was at once both amusing and annoying.

All this was under the watchful eyes of the federal police of the New South Wales government. We operated under strict protocols. At any stage, no more than two people were allowed to occupy an elevator, and the police would direct you towards the one you were meant to use. Only groups of four were allowed to enter a bus at a time, and each bus would not ferry more than a dozen people. Even to disembark required caution; three minutes had to elapse after one person had got down before the next could. You had to wear gloves at all times, sanitize your bag and wait for instructions from the police. It took us somewhere between 30 and 40 minutes to reach our respective rooms from the time our bus arrived at the hotel. Since the buses travelled in a convoy, everyone wanted to be in the last bus leaving for the ground and in the first to return to the hotel! Believe me, no one thought twice about pulling rank when it came to this.

We weren't the sole occupants of the hotel. All the Australian players and support staff who had returned with us from the IPL were also in Pullman, with Sridharan Sriram and Andrew McDonald looking after the training. One day, as we were returning to the hotel, the Aussies were leaving for practice. We waited 45 minutes in our buses for the Australians to leave, after which we were allowed to enter the hotel after due sanitization. There were days when we left for practice at nine in the morning and returned only by three-thirty or four in the evening, desperate to sink into bed.

It was in these circumstances that Siraj lost his father. We were told in no uncertain terms that when we returned to the hotel from practice, we had to remain confined to our respective rooms; we couldn't leave our room for any reason. Only Nitin Patel, the physio, was allowed out of his room to visit others for medical emergencies. When Siraj's father passed away in Hyderabad, we couldn't even go to his room and offer our shoulder for him to lean on. Nitin sat with him for a long time, trying to console him as best as he could. We had a big decision to make. Rather, Siraj had a big decision to make. If he did return to India, he couldn't come back and join the squad, given the quarantine and other constraints.

Ravi was clear that he wanted Siraj to stay back, though ultimately, that call would have to be Siraj's alone. On a zoom call, the coaching staff could only urge him to consider all possibilities. We pointed out that his father's ambition was that Siraj should play for India. My association with Siraj dates back a long time, and I kept making video calls to him every hour just to check on him. The next day at practice, everyone gave him a warm hug, and together, we prayed for his father's soul to rest in peace. A little bit of the load was perceptibly lifted from Siraj's shoulder and I believe that's the moment when the camaraderie within the group emphatically set in.

Among the things I told the boys when they trooped in in batches for fielding sessions was that on this tour, they could expect no assistance from outside the touring party. There was little scope to go out, to socialize or to catch up with friends beyond the bubble. It was imperative, therefore, that we were there for each other, that we took care of ourselves and our mates, support each other, give each other happiness. To me, the number one

thing on the to-do list was for us to be a happy group because
I believed through happiness, we could foster good performances.
A happy group invariably performs well, as the players were too
pleased to point out.

In those 14 days at Blacktown, we topped up our fitness, our
skills, played a couple of matches with the white ball and had
some simulation drills with the red and pink cherries. Finally,
on 25 November, we came out of quarantine. It was the first
time since we reached Blacktown that the families were allowed
to come out of their rooms. We were at least able to go to the
ground and let off steam; the wives and kids had no such luxury,
and they couldn't wait to leave Blacktown.

We boarded buses to move to the InterContinental Hotel
under the impression that once we finished our 14-day quarantine,
we would be treated as Australian residents for the rest of the tour.
We had been told that the same rules that applied to those who
lived in that country would apply to us, which meant we could
go out for a walk or a coffee. (Sydney was not under lockdown
at the time.) There were certain understandable restrictions, such
as avoiding large groups and indoor dining, but one could go to
an outdoor restaurant or for a walk by the beach.

Soon as we settled in our seats, the chief security officer
assigned to us by the CA pulled out a sheet of paper and a
microphone. Howard Bier, the ex-commissioner of Melbourne,
began, 'Okay, guys, I am just announcing the dos and don'ts. Once
we reach the hotel, you will notice an app on a placard. Everyone
must scan that app and enter their location when they are going
out. You cannot go out without informing the chief security
officer. You cannot hail a cab. You cannot go in a friend's car.'

Having patiently listened to this monologue, Ravi got up
from his seat in the front row, took the sheet from Bier, tore it
into four pieces and said, 'Howard, cut the bullshit and sit down.
We were told that once these 14 days were over, we'd have the

same rights as the Australian citizens. As you are dishing out this nonsense, the BCCI is talking to the CA. Do not hand over this piece of paper to any of my players. Don't board any other bus to make this announcement. I am not going to be a prisoner in my room any more, not when life is going on as per normal in Sydney. I am going out for a beer this evening, you can join me if you like.' Bier was taken aback. He could do nothing but look on in scarcely disguised disapproval when Ravi, Vikram, Arun and I sauntered to the bar later in the evening for a few beers.

By this time, we had already had six Covid-19 negative tests each; we were also getting annoyed that the goalposts were shifting for no discernible reason. That night, we did go out for a drink, though we were so knackered that we didn't even consider stepping out of the hotel. It was like celebrating our freedom after 28 days of quarantine.

By now, quarantine food had started to get boring and predictable. We reached out to a friend in Adelaide called Suman, a well-wisher of the team who entertained us whenever we visited. The Telugu-speaking Suman runs a few restaurants in Adelaide and has friends in Sydney and Brisbane who are also in the food business. The BCCI flew him down from Adelaide and put him up in a room outside the bubble, which was wonderful of them. Suman catered to all our culinary requirements, leaving everything at the concierge's by seven in the evening, from where the food would be distributed to the respective rooms. Since he wasn't in the bubble, he couldn't physically deliver the food to individual rooms; he would get tested every day to ensure all-round safety. That was a great arrangement and something for which we were truly grateful.

By the time the ODI series started, we had had just one practice session at the Sydney Cricket Ground, the day before the game. The following day, we were in the contest for only 20 of the 100 overs. After we lost the toss, Australia decided to make the most of the excellent batting conditions. By the end of the 50th over, they had raced away to 374.

As far as we were concerned, the wheels came off after the first 20–22 overs. You could visibly see the energy ebb away; the boys were in a daze, a trance-like state wherein you become like a zombie. We hit rock-bottom after the 35th over, and it got to a stage where even the best of the fielders and bowlers didn't know what was going on. They were just waiting for the end of the innings, so that they could savour some respite. The planning was far from ideal and the execution was just not there—all direct effects of the long bouts of quarantine on both sides of our Dubai–Sydney flight. Even though we had been practising and most guys had played in the IPL, playing an international game in front of a packed crowd at the Sydney Cricket Ground proved a little too much. In many ways, that was understandable. An unprecedented long layoff from practice, followed by the IPL, meant that despite their best efforts in training, the concentration levels of the boys were nowhere near where they generally used to be.

As I have mentioned earlier, the quarantine rules were such that you couldn't even meet your teammates once you left the ground. You couldn't get into a team room and have a coffee together. We didn't have team meetings. What we did was have a zoom call for fast bowlers, a zoom call for spinners. Hari Prasad Mohan, our analyst, made his presentations on the zoom call. That's why at the start of the tour, we were all over the shop. As a fielding and bowling unit, we were way below par. At one stage, it looked embarrassing, the way we acquitted ourselves on the field.

I thought at the time that Covid-19 and quarantine were perhaps a handy excuse, but I can now confidently state that it was the only reason for this team being so slipshod on the field. They looked lethargic, didn't seem to know which direction the ball was going. They were not picking up the angles; the agony goes on. After 20 overs, they didn't have the wheels in them, remnants of the long summer lockdown back in India. It wasn't like a lockdown in Australia at the time; you could still go to the park for a walk. In India, the lockdown meant you were stuck in your house.

The second ODI unfolded along similar lines. Once again, Australia threatened the 400-mark and even though we were well beaten, for the second match in a row, we had scored more than 300 in the chase. It took us those two games to even get back into the thick of things, but by the end of that second ODI in Sydney, I felt things were gradually falling in place.

Again, like at Blacktown, the support staff was knackered by this stage. We'd take the Test specialists for practice, and upon returning to the hotel, we'd attend tactical meetings of the white-ball teams. We would go to the ground for the ODIs and return late in the night, only to be confronted by the prospect of taking the Test boys to practice in the morning. We were practically managing two teams at the same time. This couldn't go on; it wasn't practical or prudent, so when we went to Canberra for the third ODI and the first two T20s, we split the support staff. Vikram, a physio, a masseur, a logistics person and two throwdown experts stayed back with the Test specialists in Sydney. The rest of us went to Canberra.

It was in Canberra that the tide started to turn. Ravi urged the team to look at the two white-ball series as a six-match showdown. His argument was that even though we had lost the first two games, we were good enough to bounce back and shade the white-ball leg 4-2. 'We are a good team, I have belief in you guys,' he told them. 'I understand it took us a while to get into the groove, but now that we are set, we will embrace the challenge of trying to win the series 4-2.' Ravi also reminded the boys how, in 2016, we lost the first four ODIs, but then rallied to win the final ODI and all three T20Is to level the white-ball contests at 4-4. 'We won four games on the bounce then, I don't see any reason why we can't do it now,' he insisted. 'We are as good as that team of 2016, if not better.'

It didn't quite pan out as per plan. Although we set out to win the remaining four games (last ODI and three T20Is), we managed to win only three of them before returning to Sydney, where Australia came back to winning ways and we split the six white-ball games 3-3. The point I am trying to make is that coming back from quarantine and jumping right into the heat of battle was anything but straightforward.

Once the limited-overs leg of the tour was done, we went to Adelaide for the day-night Test, and it was very different. The regulations were stricter and tighter, we were tested for the virus every other day. Although fans were allowed to partake of the entertainment at the Adelaide Oval, we were in a controlled bubble. There were restrictions in terms of going out, among other things, but we were quite accustomed to this by now because even though there were stringent checks and balances, there still was a certain degree of freedom.

From the disaster of 36 all out, we moved on to Melbourne for the second Test. We were all housed in one floor and dinner was served separately, so that we didn't have to interact with the other guests in the hotel. The authorities were efficient and understanding and both the teams enjoyed the experience in Melbourne. For us, the city provided greater joy because of the way we fought back after Adelaide to level the series. There was a reasonable gap before the next Test in Sydney, so we had decided to stay back in Melbourne for a few days before moving on to the next assignment.

That's when the Rohit–Rishabh restaurant incident happened. These two players, along with a few others including Prithvi and Shubman, went out for a meal. As per protocol, we could eat outdoors, but indoor dining was a no-no to eliminate closed-door contact with strangers and, therefore, minimize the risk of contracting the virus. As it turned out, it started to rain while they were eating, and so they went inside the restaurant to finish their meal.

It's impossible for Indian cricketers not to be noticed anywhere in the world. Predictably, an Indian who had gone to the same restaurant not just saw them and took pictures with them, but insisted on paying the bill too, refusing to take no for an answer. He also posted those photographs on social media, which sent the CA and the Aussie media into a tizzy. Their contention was that our players had deliberately broken the bubble.

The CA had made excellent arrangements, of that there is no doubt. It had booked a very large Qantas aircraft that ferried players from both teams and the match officials from one city to another. We never saw the face of any airport, come to think of it. We entered each airport through the back entrance. The bus drove us right to the aircraft. It was done efficiently, without any fuss.

Generally, the Indian contingent would board the aircraft first and make its way right to the back. A bunch of seats in the middle were left empty and the Australians later occupied the front of the aircraft. When we reached our destination, the Aussies disembarked and boarded their buses, and it was only when those buses left for the hotel were we allowed to deboard.

As per what had become the norm, it was us who got onto the aircraft in Melbourne first and, once we had settled down, the Australians, too, took their seats. Out of nowhere, members of the federal police force, accompanied by a steward, walked towards where we were seated, calling out the names of all the guys who had gone out for a meal when it had started raining. They were separated from the rest of us and assigned specified seats, from where they were not to budge for the duration of the flight.

In Sydney, we were placed in the strictest bubble of the Test series till then, even though there was no lockdown in the New South Wales capital. The final Test was in Brisbane, and Queensland state rules were quite strict and uncompromising. They necessitated all travellers from New South Wales to quarantine on arrival, which we weren't prepared for. We also made it clear that if the bubble rules in Brisbane were unreasonable, we wouldn't want to play at the Gabba.

In Sydney, we had a designated dining area, which we could only enter after the staff had kept the food and left. Deliveries would reach our rooms only an hour after being received at the reception, which was not ideal but which we didn't make a fuss about because we knew the stakes involved.

I was, however, a little nonplussed when I was refused entry into the elevator by an Australian paceman. He was already in the lift when I tried to get in, and he got agitated, saying, 'No, no, you can't come in. You can't enter the elevator. We have been told that we must not share the elevator with anyone from the Indian contingent.'

That was quite bizarre. We were staying in the same hotel; we were part of the same bubble; we shared space out in the middle, yet, we couldn't travel in the same elevator. What made it even more frustrating was that when we looked outside, everything seemed normal. People came in thousands to watch the match; they milled around freely, but we couldn't so much as breathe without severe scrutiny because of the Brisbane rules.

For a reasonable period of time, there was great uncertainty over whether we would go to Brisbane, where the last Test was to be played. We were very serious about not playing there if the restrictions were to remain so tight. We were initially told that it would be a hardcore bubble. Our contingent was to be accommodated in three floors, but apparently, we couldn't leave our floor to visit those in the other floors. There was to be no physical interaction among the occupants of the floors, and even food would be served in their respective floors. We were clearly in no mood to accept that.

We argued that if we stayed across three floors, we should be able to move around those floors. We needed to meet in the team room to chat, to discuss plans. In the end, they gave us a team room and we were permitted to use the fire exit to go from one floor to another. We were prohibited from using the elevator for inter-floor travel.

It was a challenge, but as a group, we decided not to talk about it after a point. We had gone there to play cricket, so we talked cricket. No one was prevented from venting or expressing his apprehensions, if any, but the players were excellent. They had their reservations, we all did, but they were not mentally affected by the off-field situations we found ourselves in. It might be a cliché, but there is an innate resilience in Indians. Having come up in tough conditions, grown up in not the most ideal conditions, they can handle challenges better than most.

I don't believe for one minute that the boys didn't want to talk about bubble fatigue because they felt it might be misconstrued as a weakness. Not at all. They coped really well, none of them was particularly uncomfortable. Yes, there were a couple of messages in our WhatsApp group about being bored, but there was no mention of bubble fatigue whatsoever.

What worked in our favour is that these guys are all good friends first and teammates later. They enjoy each other's company off the field, playing table tennis, snooker, carrom and scrabble, you name it. It helped that Ashwin's girls (aged three and five then) were there—that was great fun. They instantly lightened the mood and brought a smile to everyone's face.

That again highlighted Ravi's pre-tour contribution in making sure that the families were on board. Without family, bubble life can definitely be fatigued. It can lead to tremendous loneliness.

Sometimes, you don't want to see the same faces the entire day and then have to end up sharing evenings together, too. You want different company and towards that end, having their family around was a massive help.

The bubbles in Australia, India and later England brought the players closer than ever before. In Melbourne, in December, we started playing a game called Mafia, introduced unsurprisingly by Ashwin and then driven forward by Rohit. It had become a team game by the time we went to England later that year, with family members also joining in.

The game involves four guys being nominated as mafia, their identities not revealed, with a majority of the rest of the players being villagers. One person is nominated as a detective. There is a police force, there's a doctor. Basically, the mafia targets villagers, trying to kill them in the night to take control of the village. During the day, the villagers get together to find out who the members of the mafia are. It's a very engaging and enterprising game that brings out every facet of human behaviour and is as gripping for the players as the onlookers, of whom we had many, given the size of our travelling party. Each game would last an hour and a half and there would be mock fights and arguments. At the end, everyone would walk away beaming; their minds completely off cricket, bubble and other mundane stuff.

Once we hit the ground, though, their focus was exemplary. If there is one series where the support staff deserves credit, it was this tour of Australia. Most of the time, the support staff does its job and steps aside when the match starts; it's all about the players. But the Australian series of 2020–21 was as much about the support staff as the players. Each member of the support staff—from Ravi to the masseur—the way they kept the players in the right spirit, fresh in the mind and ready for battle, was outstanding.

If you check a video of Siraj getting his Test cap in Melbourne, you will be astonished to see who was standing beside him. Washi was not even in the Test squad, but we made sure he was in the huddle; we made sure he felt like he belonged in the squad. We didn't ask him to come just before the lunch break, which is when his services would have been required at the nets. He came to the ground with the team. In Adelaide, the bowlers' meeting was attended by Kartik Tyagi and Shardul Thakur, who were not in the team. Not once was anyone made to feel they were reserves or net bowlers—it was unbelievable. That's why when each guy got his chance to play, they already felt they were part of the team; they had already had their time under the sun.

It was perhaps in the fitness of things that our tour ended in similar circumstances in Brisbane as it had started at Blacktown. There was no housekeeping, no room service. But when you chase down 327 at a venue where Australia hadn't lost in 33 years, when you recover from being bowled out for 36 to complete a magical series triumph, it's all worth it. Believe me.

10

CRICKET DURING COVID-19
(Part Two)

'It's a virus, that's all it is.'

The flight from Brisbane to Dubai was quite the riot. Instantly, I was transported back to 2012, when we had just won the Under-19 World Cup in Australia. We were travelling commercial and I was in the last row in economy, next to the washroom. There was a lot of turbulence over the Indian Ocean and even though we had just lifted the World Cup, I could barely savour the experience. This 14-hour flight, however, was so different. We had a brand-new Boeing 777 to ourselves, just the team and our euphoric families. We cut cakes and opened bottles of champagne; it was a fabulous flight. The 14 hours rushed by in a blur.

From Dubai, we went our separate ways home for a few days of rest and relaxation, of celebrations and interviews, before re-entering bubble life. This would be our first experience of a bubble in India, and we knew we were in for a memorable ride. We quarantined for six days at the beautiful Leela in Chennai—a massive upgrade from the Australian hotels, and then got into the bubble as we began our practice sessions at the M.A. Chidambaram Stadium, where we would be playing the first two Tests against England.

On our second day of practice, Arun and I were by the side of the pitch, trying to decipher what mysteries the 22-yard strip held, when a senior official of the Tamil Nadu Cricket Association strode purposefully towards us. Both of us knew the gentleman in question very well and we also knew we were his targets, so we waited smilingly. He congratulated us on the victory in Australia and then was so overcome by emotion that he hugged the two of us! Hello, we were supposed to be in a bubble! Anyway, Arun and I quickly extricated ourselves from the hug and the delicate situation, tried to joke about maintaining social distance and quickly beat a retreat, wondering what the next month and a half had in store.

To be fair, the bubble was quite tight even though it wasn't stifling because of how well looked after we were—both teams were, truth to tell. The best part of the Indian bubble was that the staff stayed put in the hotel for the duration of the teams' stay. They didn't go home overnight. Apart from the excellent rooms and facilities, they went out of their way to ensure we had a pleasant and enjoyable stay. So, even if we were in a five-star prison, we didn't feel the constriction in our chest, like we had in Australia. Home sweet home, you might say.

It'd be no exaggeration to say that of all the bubbles I was a part of—in Australia, at home, later in England and finally in the UAE for the T20 World Cup—this was easily the best, thanks to the attention to detail and the love and affection of the hotel staff. No matter how outrageous and untimely the demand, they were delivered impeccably, immediately and with a smile. It amazed us that so many were willing to sacrifice their time with their family to make our lives easier and more comfortable and was a constant humbling reminder of our responsibility towards them and all the supporters of Indian cricket.

After the two games in Chennai, we travelled to Ahmedabad

for the remaining two Tests. We were greeted by nearly 500 people, neatly lined up on both sides of the tarmac and suitably distanced, when we landed in Gujarat. In Chennai, we had been given private entry to the aircraft, but here, we exited the airport through the normal route, though there was tight security and an unbreachable cordon in place. Beyond the cordon, we could see hundreds of people who had gathered to welcome us, though they knew that they couldn't even see anyone's face clearly because everyone was masked up. To their credit, they were all masked up, too—a grim reminder of the times we lived in.

Our first visit to the match venue took my breath away. It was my first sighting of the biggest cricket stadium in the world, the Narendra Modi Stadium, and the first day was spent basically taking a tour of the stadium, of the colosseum that doubles up as a stadium. I counted 91 steps from the dressing room to the ground and immediately wondered how difficult it would be to take the fielding kit bags up and down more than once on match day. The infrastructure is marvellous, if not the smartest. We have brought to the attention of people who matter that there is no view of the action from the dressing room, that navigating those many steps was far from ideal—after the first Test there, the boys refused to come up during tea-time, so we'd make sandwiches and protein shakes and take them to the players at ground level—but I am not sure how much can be done about all this.

The Ahmedabad bubble was as good as the Chennai one, as was the hospitality. By the time of the T20s that followed, crowds were allowed in at full capacity and to have 90,000-plus fans packing the stadium and supporting us might have been very intimidating for England. For us, it was inspirational and a further reality check not to take crowd support for granted. The atmosphere was electric, as vibrant as I have seen, and we thoroughly enjoyed ourselves. Thereafter, we went to Pune for only a week, where we were greeted by the best hotel I have stayed in—the Conrad Pune. The cricket was absorbing and despite the bubble, it's fair to say that both teams enjoyed themselves.

We had terrific team rooms in all three hotels, with a coffee maker, an ice-cream machine, a table tennis table and loads of books, though not many gravitated towards the last one. Mafia was going on in full swing in any case, and honestly, there's no strong reading culture in Indian cricket. Ashwin reads a lot, which shouldn't come as a great surprise, and Vikram is an avid reader. I read when I can, but I did find it difficult to read when I was with the Indian team; my reading did go down in those seven years. Any reading was basically either for reference or assistance from a cricketing perspective—not reading reading, if you know what I mean. I did manage to get some reading done during the Covid-19 times, especially during isolation but otherwise, it is very difficult to read on-job.

With the advent of Netflix and Amazon, reading has taken a comprehensive back seat. You can learn by watching, yes, but reading gives a totally different kick, and that too if you are physically holding a book in your hands. However, all our reference books are now on Kindle and that's only because it is impossible to lug around 1,500 pages when you travel. One of the pleasures I have rediscovered in the months since parting ways with the Indian team is finding a cosy spot, putting my feet up and losing myself in a book—any book that catches my fancy.

There was a reasonable break from cricket and bubble-life for the support staff at the conclusion of the multi-format showdown against England which ended in March 2021, but the players had no such luxury as they moved from the international bubble to the franchise bubble ahead of the IPL. Immediately at the conclusion of the IPL, we were to fly out to England for the final of the

WTC against New Zealand in Southampton. I felt for the players.

A plethora of Covid-positive tests among the squads forced the postponement of IPL 2021 midway as the second wave of the pandemic arrived. As unfortunate as the postponement was, it was a blessing in disguise as far as many of the players were concerned. They got an unexpected break to recharge themselves mentally and recoup physically ahead of a long tour to England, with the WTC final the first stop in a journey that also included five Test matches against the home side.

Of course, how could we have travelled without the attendant drama? Like it had happened eight months previously before we flew out to Australia, the days leading up to our departure from Mumbai to London were fraught with questions and uncertainty. The entire contingent with their families quarantined for 14 days in Mumbai; some of the players had brought their nannies along to look after young kids. For over a week, we weren't sure if families would be allowed to travel and even when the spouses and children were given the all-clear, the nannies' visas were rejected on a technicality. As always, the BCCI stepped in to ensure the players' interests weren't compromised and eventually the entire bunch emplaned, somewhat exhausted by the quarantine and visa challenges but buoyed that with the support cast around, the promise of a satisfying three months loomed.

The WTC was the ICC's baby, so the bubble and related arrangements fell in its ambit. Soon after we landed at Heathrow and completed the immigration formalities, we were bussed to Southampton, where we stayed at the Hilton within the Rose Bowl premises. For the first three days, we were under strict quarantine, confined to our rooms till we returned two negatives. Thereafter, we could go for practice in groups of six—five players and one member of the support staff, or four plus two sometimes. After a third negative test, we were all allowed to practise as one unit from day seven onwards.

Strangely enough, our family members, who shared a room with us, weren't allowed out of quarantine until after 11 days! Apparently, they fell under a different category and so had to return further negative tests on days eight and 11 before they could step out of the cage. There were the odd concessions, though. After the third day, they could go for a 30-minute walk, under supervision, in a secluded area with the rider that only one family could do so at a time. Families couldn't mingle or be within sight of each other.

Private security personnel, who were polite and professional, were at hand to ensure there were no protocol breaches. Apart from them, our only contact with the outside world was those from the labs who came to take our swab tests, though given that they were always masked up and nestled in PPEs (personal protective equipments), they could have been anyone!

These repeated tests were a necessary evil; we made our peace with it very early on. Some of those who came to collect samples were a little forceful, others very gentle. As a team, we decided to take it in our stride. We understood the significance of testing; we knew that was to keep us safe and protected. In any case, by the time we got to England, we each had been tested close to 90 times, so having a swab stick shoved up our nose no longer felt intrusive or out of place.

In England, we were encouraged to do self-testing. Each of us was given a box containing 21 packets. We had to open the swabs, take the sample, put it in the liquid, seal it, place it in the cover and leave it outside the door. Once we were out of the mandatory quarantine, our two excellent physios—Nitin Patel and Yogesh Parmar—would conduct the tests with help from masseurs Arun Kanade and Rajiv Kumar. We'd go over to the team room, where they would take the swab and transfer it to the liquid, which would instantly show if we were positive or negative. It is what's called the lateral flow test or rapid antigen test. All travelling family members who were confined to their

rooms had to do a lateral flow test every day and post pictures
of the result on a WhatsApp group within half an hour, so that
enough information went out to the authorities concerned that
the entire squad was Covid-19-negative.

We had a six-week gap between the end of the WTC final
and the start of the Test series against England, in Nottingham
on 4 August. Given all the restrictions in place, there was no
question of us returning to India and going back to England.
That was a logistical no-no. So after seeking the BCCI's approval,
it was decided that we would take a three-week break from the
game and go our separate ways if we so desired. In collaboration
with the England and Wales Cricket Board, the BCCI arranged
for us to stay in a hotel in London. Again, no matter where we
chose to go in that three-week period, we had to send the results
of our lateral flow test every two or three days. England had
partially opened up from 21 June and many of the restrictions
had been lifted, though it wasn't until 19 July that life as we
knew it pre-2020 returned to normal.

We weren't taking any chances. Even though there was greater
freedom of movement and fewer restrictions, we decided not to
let our guard down. We tried to lead as normal a life as possible,
which translated to some players booking castles or chalets, others
going to Scotland and staying in cottages that didn't have other
guests, and a few travelling to Cotswolds or Devon. Most of us
members of the support staff stayed back in London. For me,
the primary attraction was Wimbledon, for some of the boys, it
was Euro 2020, as it was being held a year late.

On 7 July, a week before we were to get back into the
bubble again, the BCCI had organized for the administration of
the second dose of the Covishield vaccine at the London team
hotel for those who needed it. Among those who took the second
dose was Rishabh, whom I hadn't seen for more than two weeks.
We hugged it out and spent a few moments chatting up.

On 13 July, a day before our departure from London, we all had to undergo RT-PCR tests. These revealed that Rishabh had tested positive and so had Dayanand Garani, one of our throwdown specialists and masseurs. It was a shock because we were to leave for Durham the following day for a brief camp on our way to Nottingham for the first Test. It then emerged that Arun was deemed one of Dayanand's close contacts because he had received an hour-long massage from the latter. Also identified as Dayanand's close contacts were Wriddhiman Saha and Abhimanyu Easwaran, so when we exited London the next morning, these five gentlemen were left behind to isolate for 10 days, return consecutive negative tests and rejoin the team.

Because England had opened up considerably, there was no organized bio-bubble in place. When we reached Durham, we heard that approximately one in 30 people there had Covid-19; it was a hotspot because it was a university town. Our hotel, Radisson Blu, was a throwback to the horror movies of old times; it looked unkempt and untidy, with cobwebs of various sizes competing for attention. It shouldn't have come as a surprise because we were informed that it had just reopened for operations after being shut for a year and a half.

Inside the hotel, there was a wedding, a birthday party, and a few other social events being held when we arrived. Everyone in our camp was understandably a little paranoid, but there was little we could do about it because the country had opened up. So we did what we could within our soft bubble—we decided not to use the lifts but take the stairs instead, to consciously avoid going to crowded places and ensure whenever we left our rooms, we were masked up. Those who had brought their families along were content to remain safe indoors, but it was a challenge for the bachelors in the group who wanted to go out. We had to strike a balance between the fear of getting infected and being mentally weighed down by the stress of being indoors

in a beautiful country like England for days on end, and I'd like
to think as the tour went along, we were reasonably successful
in doing so.

◼

Before we left for Durham, we were warned that there would
be plenty of rain, that Durham could get frightfully cold. To our
pleasant surprise and great fortune, there wasn't a single drop of
rain till we reached the fourteenth day of our stay. We got in
some great practice; it went down as one of the best camps in
my time with the Indian team. We worked a lot on the skill
side of things. Game plans were formulated and redrawn, and the
players adapted to them during match simulation and open nets
in preparation for the Test series.

The one man who made the most of that Durham exercise
was Rohit. From the time we hit the ground running, he was
on a mission to realign his approach towards opening the batting
in Test cricket. Much of it had to do with self-introspection. He
saw videos of how he got out to New Zealand's Kyle Jamieson
in the final of the WTC, reaching out for a ball on the fifth
stump. I don't think he liked what he saw, so he made a conscious
effort to make a significant technical adjustment that was to pay
off handsomely in the next few weeks.

Rohit worked to change the way he picked up the bat; he
worked hard on his backswing. During the whole-day camps,
he would bat before lunch as well as after lunch, making sure
that he cocked his wrist. He didn't take the bat back and away
from his body in his backlift, keeping it as close to the body
as possible, so that he either dead bats the ball or lets it go.
Once the hands go away from the body, it takes more time for
the bat to come down. It also means you have to literally go
hard at the ball. That was a huge change at that stage of his

career; the adjustment was so drastic that he almost hurt his wrist because he was cocking his top-hand (left-hand) wrist and keeping his hands close to his body, not taking them behind his body, as he would do in white-ball cricket or even as he was doing earlier in all formats.

Because of his adjustment of keeping the hands where they were in his stance, he came down softly on the ball. That allowed him to focus on timing the ball, not hitting it. It also helped him leave better. As a connoisseur and lover of Indian cricket, what stood out for me was the way he and KL left the ball in the four Test matches. That is not something you see very often in modern-day cricket, but these two worked on it. Because they let so many balls sail by, the English bowlers were forced to change their lines and bowl straighter, bowl fuller and, therefore, provide more scoring opportunities.

Has this adjustment made Rohit a little less of a white-ball opener? Maybe. But the very fact that deep down, he wanted to make a name for himself in Test cricket and was willing to put in the hard yards required to do so was brilliant. When he played in Australia in the last two Tests as an opener in 2020–21, he got out hitting shots most of the time; he was hardly out caught behind. Perhaps that also helped him come to the realization that playing too many shots at the start of the innings wasn't advisable.

The pure discipline he showed in making the change was exemplary. The most important aspect was unlearning what he had learnt. Unlearning is more difficult than learning. There is research which shows that for every wrong method one practises, they have to do the right thing at least five times to unlearn it. After that begins the process of learning something new. Also, unlearning comes a little easier maybe (I can't say from personal experience) to elite athletes because mentally, they are better at it; they can consciously unlearn. Unlearning and relearning in that Durham camp within two weeks was a phenomenal effort from Rohit.

■

Because of the Covid-19 situation, the England and Wales Cricket Board couldn't offer us warm-up games against the local county sides, so we played an intra-squad match because we had the numbers to do so. On the morning of the match, we woke to the news that Ashwin had tested positive and I got a message that I was a close contact. I was traumatized; I'd had enough of Durham and I couldn't digest the prospect of 10 more days cooped up in the same hotel room. By then, a big debate was raging in the UK on whether close contacts should isolate because a lot of people were losing their jobs on account of this. We ourselves had had a first-hand taste of the challenges of isolation—Arun was stuck in London because he was deemed a close contact of Dayanand, and even though he kept testing negative day after day (on day three, four, five, six and seven), he still had to undergo the mandatory 10-day isolation.

Not just me, Vikram, too, was considered a close contact of Ashwin, and Arun was already missing from the squad, which meant if Vikram and I had to go into isolation, the squad would be without the batting, bowling and fielding coaches. We called the BCCI and asked if we could postpone the match by at least a day when Nitin informed us that Ashwin's test result was inconclusive. Nitin took his sample again and sent it for the emergency four-hour test, while we all reached the ground in somewhat of a daze. Ashwin wasn't going to be playing the game in any case, but there was an air of unease and apprehension until, four hours later, his test came back negative and he joined us at the ground after the lunch break.

The way the players reacted on the morning of the match, when everyone was under the impression that Ashwin had tested positive, was a lesson for us—that this could happen on any morning of any Test match. How we responded to that would be the key to the result on that day and in that game. That was a great learning. We were aware that people from outside our group whom we interacted with regularly—the waiters, the janitors and the driver—were all coming from home, that there were thousands of cases in England, that anything was possible. Eventually, it did happen at The Oval, with us coaches testing positive, but the players had to go out and play. And did they play well! Although all the off-field developments must have been at the back of their minds, the way they played was amazing and their mental resilience was tremendous.

Ravi was quick to spot the misgivings of the bunch and called for a quick meeting in Durham. 'It's a virus, that's all it is,' he told us. 'Everyone is double-jabbed now. We are taking all necessary precautions. I think we need to get on with it. If you break a finger or pull a hamstring, you will anyway end up losing more than eight days, this is only 10 days. Look at Rishabh. He has come back after testing negative; he is in fine shape. Look at the positives; don't allow it to affect you mentally.

'No team has beaten Australia in Australia and England in England the same year. You have the wonderful opportunity to do so. If at all we can beat England in England, this is the team with which to do it. I want each of you to focus on the game. Everything else will come and go.'

It was a terrific little motivational speech. The message was clear: if anyone was still apprehensive about Covid-19 and wanted to leave the team and go back home, that was perfectly fine. Nothing would be held against them. After all, everyone was entitled to believe that with there being no bubble, with people coming and going and seemingly no method in place, there was a risk of contracting the virus. That's why Ravi made it clear that those who wanted to exit the side could do so without fear of repercussions, but also that those who stayed back had to remain focussed on the game. Unsurprisingly, no one took up his offer of returning home.

■

The one positive fallout of the entire situation was that because members' lounges were not in operation at the Test venues, we had bigger dressing rooms. In Nottingham, for instance, where we played the first Test, the reserves generally had to sit with the members in the stands because the dressing room was very small. This time, we got the members' lounge as the dressing room, which was just as well because the original dressing room can perhaps accommodate 15 at best and we were a group of 40! Only the support staff used the old dressing room this time around, allowing the players to bask in the luxury of the vast space that the members' lounge provided.

At Lord's, the vaunted Long Room was the common lunchroom for both teams. Who would have ever thought that? One section was earmarked for England, the other for us; stations were set up for the respective sides either side of the passage, but that didn't prevent crossover and exchange of food.

It was during this game that the spotlight was trained on Bumrah after his strategic short-ball assault on Anderson. At the end of the English innings, Bumrah walked towards Anderson to tell him he had no hard feelings; it was something that needed to be done, but Anderson shooed him away. Despite that, there was no strain in the relations between the teams. There was sledging on the ground, of course, but the English guys are not like the Aussies. Joe Root himself is very soft-spoken, Jonny Bairstow and Jos Buttler are terrific guys. Haseeb Hameed's sister is my daughter's friend. Sam Billings and Sam Curran spent a lot of time in the Indian dugout during The Oval Test, looking closely at the bats our players used. Thanks to the IPL, the cricketing world has shrunk and teams are friendly, but make no mistake, the competition is fierce when the players are out in the middle. That being said, we got a lot of good vibes from the England team, which clearly hadn't been the case in Australia.

The series was level at 1-1 after the third Test in Leeds, from where we were to travel back to London for the next game at The Oval. We had had a terrible experience on our way from London, after the Lord's Test, to the north of England. A bus journey that normally takes no more than four hours lasted almost twice as long owing to a pile-up on the motorway. We couldn't get off at the services (designated area with restaurants and washroom facilities) because of Covid-19 protocols, and because the driver couldn't drive at a stretch for more than a particular duration, he had to take a half-hour break. The euphoria of the Lord's win had evaporated by the time we trudged wearily into our hotel in Leeds. We were determined that we wouldn't risk a similar experience on the way back, so we pursued the possibility of going by train from Leeds to London.

We understood it could be a tricky logistical challenge to overcome and it was no surprise when our request was initially shot down. But then Medha Laud at the England and Wales Cricket Board somehow got the wheels rolling, so to say. She spoke to London North Eastern Railway and organized a three-compartment train only for our contingent from Leeds on the same night when the Test was to end—29 August. The train would leave Leeds at 9.45 p.m.; it was a wonderful experience and took some of the bitterness off our defeat. We reached our rooms well past midnight, but the following day was a day off. We were tested for Covid-19 and all of us returned negative tests.

On 31 August, Ravi's first book, *Stargazing: The Players in My Life*, was to be launched at our hotel. The Taj was also opening its first-ever Chambers (a new subgroup within the Taj chain of hotels) in London and, therefore, the platform was set. The Taj put on quite a show; it was the place to be in London that evening. The who's who of cricket had gathered there: Michael Holding, David Gower, Kumar Sangakkara, Dilip Doshi, Alan Wilkins and Tom Harrison, who was then the England and Wales Cricket Board's chief executive officer. Also in attendance were Harish Salve and Sam Pitroda, among others, as well as the entire Indian team. Virat and the boys came in at around 5.30 p.m., and once Ravi's and Alan's official interaction was done with, Virat spoke for a couple of minutes, after which the players left for their respective rooms.

We were there till around 8.30 p.m., catching up with the greats of the game. It was fascinating to hear Gower's thoughts on the Indian fielding. He was very keen to know about our techniques in catching. Holding held forth on Ishant's wrist position and like a sponge, I absorbed the words of wisdom that flowed from cricketing royalty.

We had a final practice session on 1 September and that evening, there was a function at the Taj honouring the Indian team of 1971, the first team from our country to win a Test series in England. Ravi, Arun and I spent no more than 15 minutes at the event because the Test was starting the following day.

The fourth Test got underway on 2 September and Ravi returned a positive test on the evening of 4 September. He had complained of back pain, a consequence of lifting a heavy suitcase, and a bit of a sore throat, but he exhibited no other symptoms. It was the third day of the game and once we got England all out, I went and sat outside in the open. Rohit was batting so well that I didn't move from my chair. After a fielding session at lunch, I came running back before the start of the play and sat on the same chair the entire day. In the evening, I felt a little soreness in my throat, so I went to Nitin, who gave me four tablets of Sinarest.

Within minutes, Nitin came to me and said, 'Sri, Arun paaji came to me complaining of cough and wheezing, and we know that Ravi has got a throat infection. I am just connecting the dots; I think it's best if the three of you get a Covid-19 test done.'

Ravi, Arun and I went to the team room with Nitin for a lateral flow test. Within two minutes, Ravi's test came back positive, while Arun and I tested negative. We went back to our respective rooms, heeding Nitin's instructions that we should isolate. The next morning, we gave another test along with the entire team, and that's the one that returned positive for Arun and me. I had no symptoms as such but was gutted that I wouldn't be able to watch the game from the ground. Little did I know then that that would be my last Test with the Indian team.

Even though I had no symptoms, the BCCI put the three of us on to the head of respiratory science at the Royal Bramford Hospital, one of UK's top hospitals. He came on a call with all three of us, allaying whatever apprehensions we might have had. My sore throat was gone in 24 hours; all I had was a bit of a blocked nose for a day. I took paracetamol for a couple of nights, some Vitamin D3 tablets, but nothing more than that.

Ravi, Arun, Nitin and I stayed back in London, while the rest of the squad travelled to Manchester for the final Test. Once they reached, Yogesh Parmar, the second physio, tested positive. He was the only physio available at the time and on the day before the match, he had treated eight or nine players because the team was on its last ounce of fuel, drained by playing back-to-back Tests with the decider looming.

When Yogesh tested positive, the players got a little agitated and tetchy, and understandably so. Anyone who was there in that room in Manchester at that point would have been petrified to play because you didn't know if or when someone else was going to test positive—in a day, two days, who knows?

I know India's decision not to go ahead with the Manchester Test didn't go down well universally, but I felt at the time, as I do now, after all these months, that it was the right decision. The players were in a delicate, if not fragile, state of mind, and this was Test cricket, not three-and-a-half hours of 20-over cricket. Speaking with the players in Manchester, I could make out how concerned they were, as much for their families as for themselves. It would have been impossible for them to focus on the cricket had the match gone on, and while I sympathize with Lancashire Cricket Club, the fans and all others, who were adversely affected by the calling off of the game, the players' interests had to come first.

While the players flew out of Manchester in batches to the UAE for the second half of the IPL, I had to quarantine till 18 September, return two negative tests and only then be eligible for the fit-to-fly certificate. I could have come out of my room on the eleventh day since I went into isolation, but the test that day also came back positive. I had to wait another three days before I returned a negative test. It was, finally, only on 19 September that all three of us coaches left London for our respective homes.

It was an unfortunate end to a cracking Test series and to our long association with Indian Test cricket. The events towards the end of the tour in London and Manchester weren't avoidable; they happened despite our best efforts and despite all the care and precautions we took. I think we were lucky to get in four Test matches. Considering how England was at the time, this could have happened in the second Test. In the times that we live in, four Tests out of five wasn't a bad bargain at all, though we would, of course, have loved to have finished off in Manchester with another overseas series win in our bag.

■

By the time we departed for Dubai on 6 November 2021 after spending a couple of weeks with our families in India, I had informed the BCCI that the T20 World Cup would be my last stint with the national team, that I would not be applying for the fielding coach's position at the' end of my tenure. Seven years was a long enough period and I thought it was time to move on to other things, though I was sure I'd terribly miss being part of the Indian dressing room; I'd miss the bonhomie and the camaraderie and the thrill of watching high-class athletes perform at their best from close quarters.

We stayed at Th8 Palm in Dubai, where the ICC had also accommodated the England team. In fact, when we reached The8 for our six-day quarantine, the Chennai Super Kings (CSK) contingent was in full force at the hotel. They had booked a whopping 106 rooms to house not just the players and the support staff but also well-wishers and supporters of the most consistent IPL franchise. As and when teams dropped out of the IPL, their players who were part of the Indian 15 were to join the team hotel, but as it turned out, because CSK went into the play-offs and beyond, the Mumbai Indians players could not move into The8 because no rooms were available!

When our squad assembled, we could see that the boys were visibly knackered. It had been very hot when they landed in Dubai in the first week of September and they were feeling the strains of the high-profile IPL and the pressures that come with entering the play-offs and making a pitch for the title. A lot of other teams also had players who had played in the second half of the IPL, but the difference was that they had four, maybe five players at most, who fell into that category, as opposed to our entire 15. Maybe the only other side that had a reasonably strong representation at the IPL were West Indies, and I am not sure if it was a coincidence that they didn't have a great World Cup either.

I was delighted to be reunited with MS, who had an interesting tournament, bursting to batting life at the right time and guiding his team to a fourth IPL crown.

I told MS that it was fabulous that he was back with the

Indian team for this tournament as mentor because he had been the captain when I first joined the team in 2014 and here he was for my last assignment, too, despite having retired as a player. Clearly, the team would benefit from his presence, but I had my own reasons to be thrilled with MS's presence—he would be there in the dressing room on my last day in office.

We had two good practice matches, against England and Australia, and two excellent practice sessions where Umran Malik, the young Jammu and Kashmir quick who had made his debut for Sunrisers Hyderabad, impressed us all. It was my first sighting of the young man in the flesh and he was really sharp, hitting the handles and the stickers and hustling and harrying the established batters. That was good to watch, from the point of view of the future of Indian cricket.

Despite the sustained tiredness within the group, we were reasonably confident going into the opening game against Pakistan. We had taken heart from our warm-up games at the ICC Academy, but we should have known better. The pitches at the Dubai International Cricket Stadium for the World Cup played differently, and once we lost two wickets in the first three overs against Pakistan, well, that was pretty much it.

We regressed further during the next game against New Zealand and were well beaten. For all practical purposes, our tournament was over even though we had three more matches to play. It was a disappointing outcome and whatever else one might say is certain to sound as nothing but an excuse.

But sitting in my living room months after the World Cup, I will say that the draw could have been better. India, Pakistan and New Zealand, the three main contenders from the group for semifinal slots—with all due respect to Afghanistan—played a triangular series in the first week of the World Cup, after which the remaining games became a bit of a formality.

A little more thought could have gone into the scheduling,

in my humble opinion. I have a feeling it was perhaps more the broadcasters than the organizers who wanted this schedule and I think they shot themselves a little in the foot. Okay, I get it, India-Pakistan was the best way to get into the tournament and was perfect as the group-opener, but Pakistan-New Zealand and India-New Zealand should have been more spaced out. Our group was pretty much done and dusted in eight days. As it turned out, India were eliminated, but it could so easily have been Pakistan or New Zealand too, which would have been grossly unfair on them as well.

Each of us could have played a match or two between our games with each other. Instead, our first two matches were against Pakistan and New Zealand, Pakistan's first two were against us and the Kiwis, and the New Zealanders' campaign started with games against Pakistan and us.

By the time we rediscovered our mojo, it was too late. When most required, we were not up to scratch. I also feel we didn't have that little slice of luck going our way. As much as I believe that the harder you work, the luckier you get, I am convinced that element of luck has to be there. When I say luck, I mean when you are doing well, there should be an opening for you in the squad, in the slot that you usually occupy. In your first match, for instance, you need a couple of things going your way—such as going out to bat at the right time. Or you need a captain who will give you that extra chance. At the end of the day, you create your luck. I use that jargon all the time as a coach with my players. But after these seven years, I do agree that you need a bit of luck in international sport, such that things beyond your control go your way from time to time.

A lot of things didn't go our way at the World Cup and it was a bit of a shame that a team that had grown to become one of the most exciting and aggressive forces in the world played some of its most timid cricket in Virat's last assignment as T20 skipper, and in the last outing for Ravi, Arun and myself with the national team. If there is a certain irony in that, I sure don't want to see it!

11

JOURNEY OF FULFILMENT

I look back on my time with the Indian team with nostalgia, fondness and the occasional regret that has more to do with the outcome than the process. As an individual, I am a better version of what I was back in 2014. As a coach, I feel more empowered, experienced and confident. The learnings have been immense and as a bonus, those seven years have given me a better standing in the society, they have given me respect.

All said and done, because the Indian team was reasonably successful during our tenure, people look up to us as coaches—to Ravi (even if he's not into full-time coaching any more), to Arun and to me. When I say people, I don't mean just the young athletes but the elite ones too, those who are already established household names. They are aware of what information we can pass on, how we can still help their careers even though we are not a part of the national set-up any longer.

Dwelling on specifics, in 2013–14, I was looking for a job outside of the NCA. I was on the threshold of joining V.V.S. Laxman's cricket academy in Hyderabad. Our negotiations were done; Laxman also offered me a 7 per cent stake in his academy if I was committed to staying on for six or seven years. The academy was Laxman's dream. He started it a little over a year after he quit the sport, so he could mould the future, and I was more than happy to be a part of his dream.

There was only one hitch—what if I got an assignment with the India or India A team in those six or seven years? Would Laxman be willing to let me go?

Understandably, Laxman wasn't. His logic was that I'd be building the academy up from scratch and if I were to leave in a year or two, the whole thing would come tumbling down. He was clear that if I accepted the contract, it would be very difficult for him to release me from it prematurely. I must say I was a little disappointed, though I could see where he was coming from.

I did believe a professional breakthrough was just round the corner for me. I had been with the team that won the Under-19 World Cup (in 2012). I was in the IPL. The feedback from most stakeholders was encouraging. I was sure a door would open somewhere, and soon. The question was where and how soon. As it were, the door was to the Indian team as its fielding coach, in the second half of 2014.

I referred earlier to my conviction of being a better coach now than I was in 2014. The philosophy of coaching has changed; it's inevitable that it will keep changing at different stages of one's coaching evolution. When you first start out, you want to be a better coach than you were the previous month, the previous year. Somewhere along the line, when you realize that you are on the right track, you want to become a professional coach. Then you want to grow in your career, you want to be successful as a coach, for people to know, recognize and respect you as a good coach. The goalpost keeps shifting, the target changes, one's own attitude and approach keep evolving.

One of the great learnings for me is the understanding that

coaching is about people, it's not about the sport at all. Of all the lessons I learnt when I was part of the Indian team—and most of those lessons have come to hit me after I left the team—this is the biggest, most significant and influential one. Convoluted as it might sound, coaching a sport is not about coaching the sport alone. It's about coaching the person, and that is my philosophy now.

The genesis for that is my belief that sport must be included as a part of one's life. And the lessons one learns from playing a team sport, specifically, makes one a better person. Without intending to sound immodest, I feel I understand the bigger picture a lot better now.

At the beginning, my focus was mainly on myself—how I could land a good coaching career, how I could be financially secure. With time, the focus started to gradually move away from me to the players I was coaching. That came with financial security; it came with having the knowledge that you have made an impact at the highest level, with your knowledge and your ability to help people be at their best to perform in the searing cauldron of international sport. There was a greater clarity in the thought process, which is a natural progression if you are committed to what you are doing.

This, in a roundabout way, brings us to the topic of Indian coaches and whether there is a willingness to invest entirely, whether we are doing enough as a country to promote our coaches. Many illustrious names have spoken passionately about this topic. I feel that quite simply, we have not done enough to encourage home-grown coaching talent.

Let's come at it from a different angle. Indian lawyers, for example, are among the best in the world. The best Indian doctors are as good as the best doctors anywhere, if not better than the best. The top Indian coaches—be it Dravid, Ravi or Arun—are as good as anyone anywhere else. In fact, they are better than most of the overseas coaches. In my opinion, there is no comparison.

Having said that, the problem is with the average Indian coaches. If you take the average of all the Indian coaches, it will be significantly lower than the average of all the English coaches or of all the Australian coaches. I think that's because most of them are not very good at putting pen to paper, and that includes some former first-class cricketers who have forayed into coaching. The players who represent India at the international level are tutored on the job, so to say, to pick up the nuances and the niceties, the etiquettes. But like me, several of the Indian coaches who played at the domestic and first-class level didn't go on to represent the country. I was a competent cricketer, a decent left-handed all-rounder, but I wasn't good enough to play for India. Likewise, if you look around the domestic cricketing landscape, you will find that close to 95 per cent of first-class coaches haven't had a taste of international cricket, for whatever reason.

Even though many of us knew our chances of wearing the country's colours were bleak to nonexistent, it didn't prevent us from investing entirely in the sport. That meant many of us quit education early on in life to pursue cricket, and I am convinced that is one of the main factors weighing down our coaches.

Cricket is a sport in which all reading material, every coaching manual, is in English. If you want to read about the sport, if you want to know more about biomechanics or communication, you can get it translated to a language of your preference, yes, but much of the impact will be lost. Whether we like it or not, cricket is a sport best articulated in English. If one is unable to understand coaching better through reading, we end up coaching mainly what we have experienced or on the basis of how we have been coached during our playing days.

The mother tongue of the average Kiwi, English or Australian coach is English, and therefore, they start with a natural but significant advantage. They can fill in the google forms and make colourful presentations; they are very good when it comes to technology, so it gives the impression that they are very good in coaching as well. Many of us aren't, unfortunately, well-versed in these processes.

If we assume that the top Indian coaches, the names I have mentioned previously, are graded as 100 on 100, the top coaches in Australia and England are perhaps 85 or at best 90 on 100. But where the average of all mid-level coaches in these countries will be 70, that of the mid-level coaches in our nation drops alarmingly to 50 or 60. Can this change? Of course it can, but it's a huge task.

It's precisely for this reason that coach education must go to every nook and corner of our country. Currently, what we are delivering as a cricket-playing nation towards educating our coaches is nothing compared to the demand. In my opinion, there is a huge gap between demand and supply.

Look at it this way. In my hometown Hyderabad alone, there are close to 200 cricket academies. At a conservative estimate, these academies taken together will cater to 10,000 trainees. On an average, each academy must have a minimum of five coaches, which means, in all, you need 1,000 coaches. Hyderabad doesn't even have 100 qualified, level-one coaches. And of those who do have the qualification, many are no longer into coaching for one reason or the other.

Essentially, in Hyderabad now, we only have 30 or 40 qualified coaches who are in charge of nearly 10,000 kids. How do they provide personal attention even if they have the expertise, which itself is debatable in many cases? Several of these kids go to private, structured academies, where the nets have got a turf pitch, an AstroTurf surface and a matting track. What are the inputs these aspirants are getting?

In a way, because of this gap, the average Indian coaching the sport doesn't go up because they have nowhere to look up to.

That worries me. And yet, take many of the Indian cricketers and ask them who their coach is or was, and it won't be a celebrated player who has represented the country with distinction.

Rishabh Pant's coach, for instance, is Tarak Sinha, who has not played first-class cricket. Rohit Sharma's early coach was Dinesh Lad, who has not even seen Mumbai colours. K.L. Rahul grew up under the tutelage of Samuel Jayaraj, who has not played for Karnataka.

My humble suggestion to all Test players aspiring for a career in coaching is simple: go to the grassroots level, develop 100 players and 25 coaches and then come and coach at the international level. It's nothing personal, and I know that will not happen. Perhaps that's why if you ask any of the current players in the Indian squad who their coach or mentor is, none of them will name a Test cricketer, an international cricketer. Why just the current team? Go back to one of the most famous names in Indian cricket. Ramakant Achrekar sir didn't play cricket at the highest level and yet he gave us Tendulkar. Keki Tarapore, Desh Prem Azad—these gentlemen didn't play for the country but have gone on to become great coaches and mentored some of India's greatest players of all time.

At present, the best coach in India is television. That's perhaps being too cynical, but I am not saying it flippantly. Fortunately, because cricket-watching on satellite television is still reasonably inexpensive in India, even a middle-class kid can afford to watch the sport on television, unlike in, England where, following the 2005 Ashes series, one has to pay top dollar for the same privilege. If you ask kids in England today what their top-five sports are, cricket is unlikely to figure in most of their lists because they don't get to watch it regularly.

Watching television can be a good learning because a lot of cricket learning is caught, not taught. It is caught when one player says something to another. It's caught when one elite cricketer talks about his experiences. It is caught when your own coach says something to another player and you happen to overhear it. Nowhere is cricket caught more than taught than in India.

■

My single-biggest takeaway from the seven years with the Indian team is that less is more, especially the higher you climb up the coaching tree.

A Japanese Zen fable I read a long while back stirred something in me and convinced me that as you progress in your coaching career, less is certainly the way to go. A young man goes to the Zen master to learn the art of Zen. The master takes him to a mountain and asks him, 'What is this?' The young student replies, 'It's a mountain.'

A decade later, the master takes his ward to the same mountain with the same question. This time, the student says, 'It's a 6,000-foot pile of mud that has limestone and granite, a lot of pebbles and a lot of stone that is not useful for construction purposes. This mountain was formed due to the convergence of two land masses several decades ago. That's why beyond a certain altitude, there is no vegetation.' Time had made the student more knowledgeable and learned, and the master acknowledged the reply with a nod.

Ten years later, the young man has become a Zen monk, and the master accompanies him to the mountain for a third time and asks, 'Now, what is this?'

The young Zen master looks intently at the mountain, turns to the master, bows his head and says, 'Master, it's still a mountain.'

That's life coming full circle, and that's what coaching is all about, too.

Initially, you don't say much because you don't know a great deal. But with time, you start learning so much, you take so much information on board. You read, write, attend courses, get accredited, stack up educational notches and embark on discourses on biomechanics, sports science and technology. There is an information overload, and that's not always the best thing.

Once you are comfortable with the knowledge you possess and have had time to process it all, you realize where the young Zen master was coming from. After 20 years, a mountain was still a mountain as far as he was concerned. Yes, it comprised graphite, minerals and limestone. Sure, there could be a volcano in it, there could be tectonic movement as well, but it is still a mountain—plain and simple. And that's where the trick lies: keeping it simple. Addition by subtraction. Taking all the trappings out and getting to the core.

I would have loved to have been a little more involved with coaching on the batting and bowling fronts when I was with the Indian team, but that wasn't possible because my focus was on fielding, and there were specialists who focussed on the other two disciplines. I feel I could have offered expertise in batting and bowling too, but my role didn't demand it, and I didn't want to poke my nose in too many things and become a nuisance to others.

Now, at my own academy, I enjoy coaching bowling as well as batting; it's such fun. It's added a new dimension to my coaching; I can do things at my own pace.

However, confidence is a double-edged sword if you allow it to mushroom into complacency. I feel a greater sense of responsibility towards these youngsters who come to learn because I know that what I teach them will make an impact on their lives going forward. I need to channel my confidence, I am acutely aware of that.

How did this confidence come about? First, I feel, from the quality of work we put in. I was there for seven years, so I will assume that we made an impact. We were not sacked; we went out on our own terms. I will take it that we delivered the goods while we were there because we were around for a long time. In our final interactions with the players at the end of our T20 World Cup campaign in November 2021, the love and respect of the team was palpable. That gave the confidence that yes, *I have done a pretty decent job.*

On our last night in Dubai, on 8 November 2021, before we left for India, Rishabh gifted all three departing coaches with a lovely Parker pen each. A lot of emotions flowed that night and it's all bit of a blur. The players later took to social media to express their feelings.

Second, thanks to the people we met and spoke to, the numerous interactions with the best of the best across the globe, my confidence levels rose. Over a drink or dinner, you get to meet top doctors, some of the greatest cricketers past and present, as well as some extraordinary writers. More often than not, you're not talking cricket, you're talking about and primarily listening to other issues beyond cricket, beyond sport. Meeting so many people—people of different cultures, different backgrounds, different positions and different walks of life engaged in varied pursuits—you learn so much.

I am beyond excited as I embark on the next innings of my professional career with Coaching Beyond, an endeavour that's close to my heart. My wife Vijayalakshmi is delighted that I come home every evening from work, that our conversations aren't on WhatsApp video or FaceTime any longer. I am getting to eat home food regularly, though I have made a conscious effort to keep a watch on my weight. I have a first-class gym at my academy and the S&C and physio ensure I don't overindulge.

At some stage in the future, I'd love to be reassociated with the IPL, but there is enough at Coaching Beyond to keep me invested and occupied.

What is Coaching Beyond, you ask? It's something that has actively occupied my mind for the last four or five years, but the Covid-19 lockdown allowed me time to conceptualize and register it. I've always wanted to create something that would stand the test of time in terms of an environment that is to conducive to learning. You must create an ecosystem where the learning is so good that you don't have to worry about winning or creating champions because such things are organic and inevitable.

The idea is to create an atmosphere where a young boy or girl comes to train and goes back a good person. Whether they choose to pursue cricket as their career, or they choose some other sphere, they should come out as confident individuals, learning more than just the sport. That was my dream, and I shared my views and philosophy with Ravi and Arun. Fortunately, they both were on the same page as well and we decided we wanted to do something for grassroots and semi-professional junior athletes who can go on to become the best versions of themselves.

We feel we can use our experience to help them bridge that gap. Sticking with Hyderabad as an example, there are so many good cricketers who don't know how to bridge that gap between knocking on the doors of Ranji Trophy and becoming an elite cricketer. It's pure luck that Arun came on board as coach of the Hyderabad Ranji team in the 2016–17 season and helped Siraj realize his true potential. Had that not happened, who knows where he would be today.

During the early part of my coaching career, for the first half-a-dozen years or so, I never believed in luck. I belonged to the school which held that the harder you worked, the luckier you got. But as I grew into my role, I came to accept that luck, timing, destiny, fate or whatever you may to call it, is important too. Along with hard work and total commitment, you need the stars to align. Siraj was working as hard as he could, but it was only when Arun came on board that he found direction. It was only then that he could channelize his focus and combine hard work with smart work. Merely putting in the yards at practice isn't enough, no matter what anyone might tell you. You can't take a donkey and make it into a horse, for instance. You can make a donkey a better donkey but never a racehorse. Likewise, you treat a racehorse like a racehorse, otherwise it will simply stagnate and fail to realize its full potential.

Our Hyderabad centre of Coaching Beyond is a pilot project. Essentially, the institute has three verticals. The first is brick-and-mortar cricket academies. We have pilot projects of Coaching Beyond in Hyderabad and Chennai purely because I live in Hyderabad and Arun, in Chennai.

The second vertical is what I have alluded to earlier, coach education. Now, this is the real baby of Coaching Beyond. We will have an online coach coaching accreditation programme, which will be of gold standard. It is being done by Arun, myself and Dr Kinjal Suratwala, who was the head of coach education of the BCCI for 10 years. I first ran into him when he was at the NCA and since then, he has evolved exponentially.

Between us, we realized the mistakes we had made during our level one, two and three coaching courses. Coaching has completely changed now, and we are in a better position to understand how it should not be, as much as how it should be. We are aiming to create a coaching community. When you are conducting coaching courses, you connect with many other coaches. Our curriculum involves giving those who do an online course the opportunity to come and coach at our place, to back up theory with practical experience and knowledge.

Learning coaching is a slow and gradual process; you cannot become a coach in six days. You will only be eligible to think of yourself as a coach when you have coached day in, day out for five years in a row. We will have to provide coaches the chance to encounter new ideas and learn from others, as well as benefit from closely observing how master coaches go about their business. It's what I like to call 'informal learning'.

Yes, you can get a coaching certificate or call it a licence through an online programme, but informal learning is arguably even more important. Of course, formal qualification is a must, but that's only 10 per cent of the entire deal. Informal learning, which contributes almost 90 per cent to one's growth as a coach, is not in the curriculum.

What's the difference between formal and informal learning? Informal education is constant learning because it provides you with a different challenge every day. The real learning takes place on the ground; it doesn't happen on the concrete floor of a classroom. When you are working day in, day out, week after week, with real players, in the real environment, that is where true learning happens. That is what we are providing coaches now.

Many former cricketers from across the country express their interest to come over and pursue a one-year internship, which is the informal learning we wish to provide because we want them to come here and develop their knowledge. We'll teach level one, but the coaches need to develop their own style, do it in their manner.

One of our other areas of focus is creating a work-life balance. Coaching is a very demanding profession. Whether one is doing it as a volunteer or professionally, it's highly demanding and stressful. To be very honest, some of the young coaches' first question is what the financial package is, and I am not sure that's the right way to go about it. If you see all the best coaches, they're never in it only for the money.

Money is important, I am not disputing that, but it should not be the driving force. Coaching should not be an excuse in the pursuit of quality living because when you're coaching, it gives you a sense of satisfaction that few other professions do. Coaching is probably one of the most undervalued professions globally. No matter how much effort you put in, there'll always be a dozen parents who are upset. They will feel you've not done enough with their kids. And, you have to be at your best with every single player who comes to you. Frankly, that is not humanly possible every single day. That's what I mean when I say coaching is undervalued and extremely demanding.

That's why at Coaching Beyond, we try to create a good work-life balance. How to delegate, how to manage your time, how to take care of your own self, how to manage your family time, how to manage your logistics—these are some of our key focus areas at the institute. It's a holistic process; it's not just about the cricket. We don't discourage coaches from copying ideas; learning and looking for inspiration from other projects is heavily recommended by researchers. It is okay to take a design or batting drill from other coaches or from the internet, but you need to suit it to the context of your player.

The best way to learn is by interning under a master coach for a good period of time. Creating at least 50 to 60 good coaches in the next three to four years is our immediate target.

The third vertical will be a follow-up of the second, which is a franchise model. Once we have 60 to 70 good coaches on our roster, we will have many more centres of the kind that already exist in Hyderabad and Chennai, running the same kind of programmes with the same intensity and speaking the same language.

Another passion of mine is to make coaching a full-time subject, a full-time occupation. In India, sport has attained a high level of professionalism, but how many coaches are professionally involved only in coaching? We have 14 coaches at Coaching Beyond in Hyderabad, but only two of them are full-time. Everybody else is either in the railways, in banks or in government service. Because they hold jobs, they are only able to devote say two or three hours in the morning and maybe as much time in the evening.

They are what I call time-poor coaches. Because they don't have the time, they can't make programmes, they can't be creative. They can't go online and learn and, therefore, it's harder for them to open up to the possibilities that exist. We need to make coaches rich in time because only then can they pursue coaching without obstacles and roadblocks. I knew I was taking a big risk when I left State Bank of Hyderabad, but had I not done so, I would have been a time-poor coach who would have done little justice either to my bank job or my pursuit of coaching.

One of the advantages of going the franchise route is that more students will benefit from it. Today, in Hyderabad, we have 15 coaches including me and 150 trainees, a ratio of 1:10. If we have 50–60 coaches, nearly 600 kids across the country will benefit. That's how we need to take quality coaching forward while maintaining the balance between explicit and informal learning for the children also.

Too much structured coaching is also not good because most of our cricketers come from an unstructured learning environment. We'll have to maintain that balance, that's a big challenge, but I am confident we will be able to first initiate and then sustain that to the best extent possible.

■

If I have been able to embark on my preferred journey of making a career out of coaching, it's entirely due to the support I have got from home.

I am lucky that my mom is a huge cricket buff, which is why she allowed me to play cricket even if it was at the expense of academics. That was a big plus, given our conservative middle-class background. When we got married, my wife, Vijayalakshmi, knew very little about cricket, but she backed me in my endeavours, always with a smile and never giving me the impression that she was anything but fully behind me. She wasn't demanding or insistent that I devote more time to her at the expense of cricket.

I am extremely fortunate to have such an understanding wife. Be it when it came to quitting my bank job or quitting the NCA and joining Kings XI Punjab for a low financial package, she was solidly behind me, giving me the freedom to chase my dream. I can't even imagine how difficult it must have been for her. When our daughter was growing up, I was barely home. Since 2008, I was with the NCA and would spend more than half the year in Bengaluru while my family was in Hyderabad. By 2010, my time away from home had increased to almost nine months a year, which is when we decided that my daughter and wife should move to Bengaluru. But even when we were all together in Bengaluru for three years, I was away for long periods. I salute her for having had the courage and fortitude to bring up our young daughter practically on her own.

I hardly saw my child growing up, but that's not a complaint. It was a choice I made; it was a choice we made as a family because that's the only way it can work. Family is paramount, it always comes first. No matter what you might do or who you might be, there is nothing more fulfilling than going back to your family at the end of the day. I'd almost forgotten that feeling for more than a decade, so I appreciate my wife's sacrifices all the more now.

Every positive has a negative, as Duncan Fletcher often used to say. The positive for me is that my job gave me the security to take care of my family. If I am able to invest 12 hours a day to Coaching Beyond, knowing well that I won't make a single rupee for the next two years because I am investing in my dream, that's because of the financial security I've got by being able to do what I did with the BCCI for the last 10 years. The negative is that I didn't see my daughter grow up. I have learnt more about her in the few months since the end of my tenure with the Indian team than in the decade and a half preceding it. Sadly, now that I am back home, she's all set to leave the nest and jet off to university. I reiterate, that's not a complaint, it's just a peek into the life of a professional who makes choices that might not be ideal but are essential.

Sometimes, we tend to take family for granted. I have nothing but the greatest admiration and respect for mine. Ours is a small, tight-knit family. My older brother Murali is a dedicated armchair critic who watches all sport and is particularly fascinated by the twists and turns of Indian cricket. Having been away in Abu Dhabi for nearly 20 years, he is back in Hyderabad following the end of his stint with Etisalat as their vice president of sales and marketing. In my formative years, he and my mother encouraged me to plunge wholeheartedly into cricket. They have been as much pillars of strength as Vijayalakshmi and my daughter. That's something I am eternally grateful for.

ACKNOWLEDGEMENTS

I would like to thank and acknowledge all those who helped conceive, conceptualize and deliver this dream of mine to you.

To all those who encouraged me to start writing, read drafts and offered suggestions for improvement.

To Vijju, my dear wife, and my daughter Ananya, who both patiently walked the journey with me.

To Kaushik, who transformed my thoughts into a structured narrative and coaxed old memories and facts out of me over the many months we worked together on the book.

To Rupa Publications, Kapish, and of course, Rudra, for his patience and for putting up with my persistent delays in proofreading.

To Manali, for her commitment and care in ensuring we get everything as right as possible.

And finally, to all my friends, fans and cricket lovers, who have been my constant source of support through triumph and tribulation.